The Annotated Plutarch
Pericles

Plutarch's Lives Made Easy

with the

Annotated Plutarch Series

Original text by Plutarch
Annotated and Expanded by Rachel Lebowitz
Translation by George Long and Aubrey Stewart

Published by A Charlotte Mason Plenary, LLC

Published by A Charlotte Mason Plenary, LLC

The Annotated Plutarch
Pericles
The Annotated Plutarch Series
Volume 2
2nd Edition

Text by Plutarch and Rachel Lebowitz
Annotated and edited by Rachel Lebowitz
Translation by George Long and Aubrey Stewart

Issued in print and electronic formats.
ISBN: 978-1-954822-14-6 (paperback)

A Charlotte Mason Plenary is an educational company committed to furthering the ideas and educational philosophy of Charlotte Mason. We specialize in customizing curricula for families. We offer books, study guides, courses, and homeschooling consultations, including special needs consultations, based on the Charlotte Mason method of education.

Visit A Charlotte Mason Plenary at
CMPLENARY.COM

The Annotated Plutarch

Pericles

Plutarch's Lives Made Easy
with the
Annotated Plutarch Series

Table of Contents

PREFACE

Preface to Plutarch's Lives

Plutarch just got a whole lot easier! And more fun too! Thank you for choosing The Annotated Plutarch Series from A Charlotte Mason Plenary.

Why Study Plutarch?

Plutarch was a Greek historian who lived c. 45-120 CE. He is known as the very first biographer. He wrote biographies of Greek and Roman men in his book *Lives of the Noble Greeks and Romans*. But he didn't just write about the accomplishments of these men, he also wrote about the smaller happenings of their lives in order to give us a glimpse into their characters. This is why Charlotte Mason included Plutarch in her curriculum. It is about evaluating character.

What makes a person great? What makes a person weak? What makes a tyrant? Plutarch shows us that it is the small decisions in a man's life that make up his character. We then get to see the consequences of those decisions. Plutarch does not judge for us. He lays the man's life before us and we are left to judge. It truly is a remarkable way to study character and morality.

Charlotte started her students in Citizenship Studies in Form 2B, or about 4th grade. The student spent a whole year reading *Stories from the History of Rome* by Beesly. This prepared the student for Plutarch by providing the context of Ancient Roman society. Then in Form 2A, or about 5th grade, the student started reading one of Plutarch's *Lives* every term. This is the foundation of her character and citizenship teaching. It is not to be missed.

How to Use The Annotated Plutarch Guides

This Annotated Plutarch Guide comes with the original text translated from the Greek. You do not need to purchase anything else to study Plutarch.

There are several sections written by The Plenary to help the student:

- The Introduction gives you biographical information about Plutarch himself.
- A "Who's Who" is included to help you understand the key players in this Guide.
- A Prologue sets the scene and will give you essential background information to begin your study.
- The Epilogue wraps up the Study Guide, connects it to more modern events, and gives the student some important ideas to think about.

Other lessons include the original text by Plutarch. Just as Charlotte Mason used edited versions of Plutarch's *Lives* for her students, this text has been edited for content and length for your student. Anything unsuitable for students has been removed. You can feel comfortable about handing this Plutarch Guide to your student for independent use.

For ease of reading, the original text is in the inner column and added annotations are in the outer column. The annotations define vocabulary words and phrases and include pronunciations. The annotations also provide context to allow you to fully understand Plutarch's frequent references to the people, places, and culture of ancient Greece and Rome. **All annotated words are in bold type**. The goal is to highlight the text so that readers may gain a deeper understanding of it for themselves.

Translation

The Plenary uses the translation by George Long and Aubrey Stewart for most of our Plutarch Study Guides. The Long

translation is easier and more accessible for today's students, which will make the subject of Plutarch easier for you and your students.

We chose not to use the translation by Thomas North because it is a second translation of an earlier French translation done by Jacques Amyot in 1559. A translation of a translation is too far removed from the author's original words.

Long and Stewart translated Plutarch's *Lives* from the original Greek. This makes the Long translation more accurate.

George Long was a professor of Greek and Latin at University College in London. He was a major contributor to *Smith's Dictionary of Greek and Roman Antiquities*, and also wrote for the companion Biography edition. Aubrey Stewart was a Fellow at Trinity College in Cambridge, England. Together, they translated Plutarch's Lives from the original Greek into several English volumes in the 1880s.

Plutarch Resources and Picture Study

In addition, as you read through the Guide, you will find references to other resources that connect to Plutarch's story. These include classic paintings, poems, and other items that help further illustrate the text. It is my intent to provide you with these additional resources to bring your Plutarch study to life.

All of the additional resources are free and can be found on the Plutarch Resources page of The Plenary website. I encourage you and your students to take advantage of these additional resources.

If you would like high resolution images, printed copies of the paintings, and additional background information on each painting, we also offer a Plutarch Picture Study for each Guide.

The accompanying Plutarch Picture Study helps students connect Plutarch's text to classical paintings by famous artists. Artists across the ages have illustrated the fascinating stories found in Plutarch's Lives. The Picture Study also includes study questions about the text and the artwork to help students make a deeper connection.

For more information regarding the Resources Page and the Picture Study for this Guide, go to:

CMPLENARY.COM/PLUTARCH-RESOURCES

A Thank You

I hope The Annotated Plutarch Series makes Plutarch more accessible and more fun for you and your family. I sincerely hope you come to love Plutarch as much as I do!

Sincerely,

Rachel Lebowitz
A Charlotte Mason Plenary

Introduction

Plenary Introduction

Who was Plutarch?

Plutarch, or Plutarkos in Greek, was an ancient Greek historian and philosopher. He is most well-known for his two works, *Parallel Lives* and *Moralia*. Plutarch lived in the little town of Chaeronea, Greece, from approximately 45-120 CE. His family appears to have been well-established there and his father was also an author and philosopher. From several passages in Plutarch's writings, we know that he studied at the Academy of Athens, which was founded by Plato.

Plutarch /PLOO-tark/

But the most important event in his life was his journey to Rome. It was during this time that Plutarch officially became a Roman citizen and changed his name to **Lucius Mestrius Plutarchus**. During this trip he did most of his research that would later become his book, *Lives of the Noble Greeks and Romans*, commonly known as *Parallel Lives*. Plutarch published the biographies as pairs, one Greek life with one Roman life, in an attempt to compare and contrast the two lives for their virtues and their failings. For example, the *Life of* ***Publicola***, a Roman Aristocrat, is paired with the *Life of Solon*, a Greek Athenian, both of whom were Statesmen.

Lucius Mestrius Plutarchus /LOO-shus MES-tree-us ploo-TARK-us/

Publicola /pub-LIH-cō-luh/

Plutarch's *Lives* has been preserved through the centuries and has been translated from the original Greek into many other languages. The first translation from the original Greek was done in French by Jacques Amyot in 1559. Just 20 years later, Thomas North published the first edition in English. North did not translate directly from the Greek, but instead used Amyot's French translation to publish it in 1579. North's English edition immediately became very popular in England during the reign of Queen Elizabeth I. Shakespeare used North's edition as source material for some of his historical plays, including *Julius Caesar*,

Antony and Cleopatra, and *Coriolanus*, as well as references to Plutarch's *Life of Theseus* for *A Midsummer Night's Dream*.

Plutarch's influence spanned beyond England as well. People have always read Plutarch. His readers include George Washington, Thomas Jefferson, Alexander Hamilton, Benjamin Franklin, Abraham Lincoln, Ralph Waldo Emerson, and Theodore Roosevelt, just to name a few.

But why should *we* read Plutarch? What does the modern student gain from reading such an ancient text? What can we learn from a man who lived so long ago? Only a few of the men he wrote about are still known to us, such as Julius Caesar or Alexander the Great. Most of the names represented in Plutarch's *Lives* are completely unknown to the contemporary culture of today. Even Plutarch himself is not well-known except among scholars. So why read his stories?

Although Plutarch himself belongs to the ancients, his lessons are timeless. He was more concerned with documenting men's characters than their deeds, and *that* is what we have to learn from Plutarch: the value of discerning character.

Plutarch was quick to point out that he wrote *biographies*, not histories. In his *Life of Alexander*, Plutarch stated that a man's character is often revealed in subtle ways:

> "a man's most brilliant actions prove nothing as to his true character, while some trifling incident, some casual remark or jest, will throw more light upon what manner of man he was than the bloodiest battle, the greatest array of armies, or the most important siege. Therefore, just as portrait painters pay most attention to those peculiarities of the face and eyes, in which the likeness consists, and care but little for the rest of the figure, so it is my duty to dwell especially upon those actions which reveal the workings of my heroes' minds, and from these to construct the portraits of their respective lives, leaving their battles and their great deeds to be recorded by others."

Did You Know? Even fictional characters in literature have been known to read Plutarch! The monster in Mary Shelley's book, *Frankenstein,* finds a bag of books, one of which is Plutarch's *Lives of the Noble Greeks and Romans*. It is from this book that the monster learns about the idea of *character*.

And it was in his intro to the *Life of **Timoleon*** that he wrote:

Timoleon /tuh-MŌ-lē-un/

> "It was for the sake of others that I first undertook to write biographies, but I soon began to dwell upon and delight in them for myself, endeavoring to the best of my ability to regulate my own life, and to make it like that of those who were reflected in their history as it were a mirror before me. By the study of their biographies, we receive each man as a guest into our minds, and we seem to understand their character as the result of personal acquaintance, because we have obtained from their acts the best and most important means of forming an opinion about them. What greater pleasure could'st thou gain than this? What more valuable for the elevation of our own character?"

Quotes are from *Plutarch's Lives: Translated from the Greek* by Aubrey Stewart, M.A., and George Long, M.A., Volume 1, published in 1844.

Character–other people's and *our own*. That is what Plutarch urges us to consider.

Who's Who
in Plutarch's Life of Pericles

Pericles	Statesman of Athens, Greece; lived from approximately 495-429 BCE
Lampon	a soothsayer and interpreter of oracles
Thucydides, son of Melesius	Athenian statesman; head of the Conservative party of Athens and rival to Pericles
Thucydides	Greek historian who wrote *History of the Peloponnesian War*
Phidias	famous Greek architect and sculptor; friend of Pericles
Callicrates and Ictinus	Greek architects who built the Parthenon under the supervision of Phidias
Anaxagoras	a Greek scientist and philosopher; Pericles' teacher
Cimon	Athenian statesman; a rival to Pericles
Tolmides	Athenian General during the Peloponnesian War
Lamachus	Athenian General during the Peloponnesian War
Pleistoanax	King of Sparta during the Peloponnesian War
Cleandridas	Spartan General during the Peloponnesian War
Aspasia	Pericles' second wife
Socrates	Greek philosopher known as the founder of Western philosophy

Lesson 1
The Golden Age of Athens

Lesson 1

The Golden Age of Athens

"The period which intervened between the birth of Pericles and the death of Aristotle is . . . the most memorable in the history of the world."
- Percy Bysshe Shelley

"Freedom was a Greek discovery" says Edith Hamilton in her book *The Echo of Greece.* She continues with this story: Once an Athenian army, far from home and surrounded by greatly superior forces, had to try to break through them as a last chance. Their leader made a short speech before they started. "You live," he told them, "in the only free city in the world. In Athens alone the state does not interfere with a man's daily life." (pg 12)

So said Pericles to his soldiers.

In the fifth century BCE, Athens rose to power under the leadership of one man: Pericles. This small span of one-hundred years of the city's prosperity is still known to us today by two interchangeable phrases: "The Golden Age of Athens" is also "The Age of Pericles."

But the story of Athens begins centuries before the birth of Pericles. This is a city whose influence can still be seen and felt in our modern world. What made this ancient city so special?

To know Athens is to know the Greek goddess **Athena**. According to legend, the city was first ruled by a king named **Cecrops**, who made the city so beautiful that it caught the attention of the Greek gods on Mount Olympus. Both **Poseidon** and Athena fought over the honor of being the city's protector, as described in *The Story of Athens* by Howard Butler:

"Their struggle took the form of a contest before a jury of the gods of Olympus, in which each strove to produce the gift which

Athena was the Greek goddess of wisdom and war, as well as arts and crafts. She was the daughter of Zeus. Athena plays a key role in both the *Iliad* and the *Odyssey* by Homer. She is referred to as *Minerva* in Roman mythology.

Cecrops /SEE-krops/ was the first king of Athens. Some say he was a real king; others say his story is simply a legend and that he was half man, half serpent or fish.

Poseidon was the Greek god of the sea, earthquakes, storms, and horses. He is very ill-tempered. He is also referred to as *Neptune* in Roman mythology.

CMPLENARY.COM You can see a painting that depicts the battle between Athena and Poseidon on the CMP website.

PLUTARCH PICTURE STUDY See Print #1 in the Plutarch Picture Study for Pericles.

should be most useful to mortals. The scene of the contest was the Acropolis.

Poseidon, having the first turn, struck the rock with his mighty trident, causing a spring of salt water to gush forth, and leaving three marks which are still to be seen in the Acropolis rock. At the blow, forth leaped the first horse, with all his strength and fleetness, ready to become the faithful servant and companion of man.

Athena then, in her turn, with no show of brute strength, fashioned the homely olive tree and described all its possibilities of usefulness to humankind.

And though Poseidon's gift has perhaps proved the more useful to the greater number of the sons of men, it was certainly more in keeping with mortal sentiment in those days that the gods should award the victory to Athena. She became from that moment the protectress of Cecropia, and the city exchanged its original name for hers.

This judgement of the gods was a fortunate one for the Cecropians. The worship of Athena, preeminent from that time upon the Acropolis, the love and enthusiasm for their divine protectress which animated the inhabitants of the newly named city, seem to have molded all their subsequent history and directed their destiny during all the succeeding ages. The stately form of Athena, her courage, her chastity, can be traced in all the dignity of their political career, in their deeds of valor, and in the purity of their ideals in literature and art.

Metis /MEE-tis/ was a Greek Titan and the mother of Athena. She was known as the goddess of wise counsel, deep thinking, and cunning.

Athena, daughter of Zeus, the most powerful, and of ***Metis****, the wisest of the gods, represented to the Greeks a harmonious blending of might and wisdom. As offspring of Zeus, she represented government, a protectress of the state; as a daughter of Metis, she symbolized the authority of law. As goddess of war, Athena became the protectress of the state against foreign enemies and led the Athenians to many a victory on the field of battle.*

Eros, also known as *Cupid*, was the Greek god of love.

She was, moreover, a virgin goddess, against whose breast the arrows of ***Eros*** *were shot in vain. Patron of valor in men and chastity* *in women, she stood before the youth of Athens an example of the highest ideals in life, a unique figure in the Olympian hierarchy.*

Besides being foremost in the line of battle, waging almost ceaseless wars, Athena was patron of the fine arts and of the domestic accomplishments of weaving and the like. From her creation of the olive tree she was considered a protecting deity of agriculture, and was believed to have given the plow and the olive-press to her devotees in Athens. The serpent, the owl, and the olive tree symbolized her respective attributes, and were sacred to her throughout Greece.

Can it be doubted that the worship of so high an ideal was largely instrumental in placing Athens at the political head and center of Greece, in making her orators and statesmen preeminent in the ancient world, in establishing her schools of philosophy as the first and greatest of antiquity, in producing sons foremost in valor, first in peace, and in developing her art to a level of priority for the whole world?" (pgs 10-12)

Hundreds of years after the founding of Athens, Pericles would honor the goddess Athena with a building project that still stands today.

How did one man's life so alter the course of a city, a state, and, ultimately, Western Civilization?

Edith Hamilton says, "In the fifth century BCE, Athens showed what free men living and working together can bring to pass . . . To all Greeks, freedom was first in importance. Fundamental to everything the Greeks achieved was their conviction that good for humanity was possible only if men were free, body, mind, and spirit, and if each man limited his own freedom. A good state or work of art or piece of thinking was possible only through the self-mastery of the free individual, self-government." (pg 29)

In his ***Life of Solon***, Plutarch describes the "Greek discovery of freedom" and the idea of a government based on a democracy. After all, the word democracy is a word with two Greek roots: *'demos,'* meaning *the people*, and *'kratos,'* meaning *power* or *rule*.

Plutarch also wrote about **Solon**, a Greek statesman who lived c. 630-560 BCE.

He continues the story of the Athenian quest for self-governance in his *Life of Pericles*. But he does not begin with a story about Pericles. Instead, Plutarch delivers several small tales regarding the emulation of virtue as his opening scene. One might venture a guess as to why Plutarch begins this way, for, according to an ancient historian, Pericles once said,

> *"Where the rewards of virtue are greatest, there the noblest citizens are enlisted in the service of the state."*

Plenary Discussion Questions

1. What do you think about the two gifts offered by Athena and Poseidon? Which do you think was the better gift? Why?
2. Name some things you learned about the Greek goddess Athena.
3. What does *democracy* mean? What are the Greek roots of the word and how does that apply to the definition that we give the word *democracy* today?
4. Why do you think Plutarch starts his *Life of Pericles* with a tale about emulating virtue?

Lesson 2
Plutarch's Introduction

Lesson 2

Plutarch's Introduction

One day in Rome, **Caesar**, seeing some rich foreigners nursing and petting young lapdogs and monkeys, enquired whether in their parts of the world the women bore no children: a truly imperial reproof to those who waste on animals the affection which they ought to bestow upon mankind. May we not equally blame those who waste the curiosity and love of knowledge which belongs to human nature, by directing it to worthless, not to useful objects? It is indeed unavoidable that external objects, whether good or bad, should produce some effect upon our senses; but every man is able, if he chooses, to concentrate his mind upon any subject he may please. For this reason, we ought to seek virtue, not merely in order to contemplate it, but that we may ourselves derive some benefit from so doing. Just as those colors whose blooming and pleasant hues refresh our sight are grateful to the eyes, so we ought by our studies to delight in that which is useful for our own lives; and this is to be found in the acts of good men, which when narrated incite us to imitate them.

Caesar refers to Caesar Augustus (63 BCE – 14 CE), born as Gaius Octavius Thurinus, who was the first Emperor of the Roman Empire.

The effect does not take place in other cases, for we frequently admire what we do not wish to produce; indeed, we often are charmed with the work, but despise the workman, as in the case of dyes and perfumery which we take pleasure in, although we regard dyers and perfumers as vulgar artisans. A clever saying of **Antisthenes**, who answered, when he heard that [a certain man] was a capital flute player, "But he must be a worthless man, for if he were not, he would not be such a capital flute player!" And **King Philip of Macedon**, when his son played brilliantly and agreeably on the harp at an entertainment, said to him, "Are you not ashamed, to play so well?"

Antisthenes /an-tĭs-thĭ-neez/ (445-365 BCE) was a Greek philosopher. When he was young, he was so eager to be a student of Socrates that he walked more than 5 miles from his home to the city of Athens each day. He became such a beloved student of Socrates that he was even present at the Socrates' death.

Philip of Macedon (382-336 BCE) was king of the northern Greek region of Macedonia. His son was Alexander the Great.

It is enough for a king, if he sometimes employs his leisure in listening to musicians, and it is quite a sufficient tribute from him to the **Muses**, if he is present at the performances of other persons.

If a man devotes himself to these trifling arts, the time which he wastes upon them proves that he is incapable of higher things. No well-nurtured youth, on seeing the **Statue of Zeus at Olympia**, wishes that he were a **Phidias**, for it does not necessarily follow that we esteem the workman because we are pleased with the work. For this reason men are not benefited by any spectacle which does not encourage them to imitation, and where reflection upon what they have observed does not make them also wish to do likewise; whereas we both admire the deeds to which virtue incites, and long to emulate the doers of them.

We enjoy the good things which we owe to fortune, but we admire virtuous actions; and while we wish to receive the former, we wish ourselves to benefit others by the latter. That which is in itself admirable kindles in us a desire of emulation, whether we see noble deeds presented before us, or read of them in history. It was with this purpose that I have engaged in writing biography and have arranged this book to contain the lives of Pericles and of **Fabius Maximus**, men who especially resembled one another in the gentleness and justice of their disposition, and who were both of the greatest service to their native countries, because they were able to endure with patience the follies of their governments and colleagues.

The **Muses** were the Greek goddesses of the arts who inspire all poetry, song, and dance. There are nine Muses, all daughters of Zeus.

CMPLENARY.COM See a rendering of what Phidias' ***Statue of Zeus at Olympia*** might have looked like on the Pericles Resources Page at: cmplenary.com/plutarch-resources/pericles

Phidias /Fĭ-dee-us/ (490-430 BCE) was a Greek sculptor, painter, and architect. His *Statue of Zeus at Olympia* was one of the seven wonders of the world.

Quintus Fabius Maximus (280-203 BCE) was a Roman general who fought against Hannibal. He was one of the first to use the tactics now known as guerilla warfare.

Plutarch always paired two *Lives* to compare and contrast their virtues and weaknesses. In this case, Pericles is paired with Fabius Maximus.

Plenary Discussion Questions

1. What do you think about the opening story of Caesar and his disdain for foreigners with pets?
2. Plutarch says "If a man devotes himself to trifling arts ... he is incapable of higher things"? Do you agree with him? Why or why not?
3. "Men are not benefitted by any spectacle which does not encourage them to imitation." Do you agree? Why or why not? Can you think of any 'spectacle' which benefits mankind?
4. Why did Plutarch decide to write *biographies* rather than history?

Lesson 3
Who Was Pericles?

Lesson 3

Who was Pericles?

Pericles was of the tribe **Akamantis** and was descended from the noblest families in Athens, on both his father's and mother's side. His father, **Xanthippus**, defeated the Persian generals at **Mykalé**. His mother, Agariste, dreamt that she had brought forth a lion, and a few days afterwards was delivered of Pericles. His body was symmetrical, but his head was long and out of all proportion; for which reason in nearly all his statues he is represented wearing a **helmet**, as the sculptors did not wish, I suppose, to reproach him with this blemish. The poets called him squill-head, and the comic poet, Kratinus, in his play *Nemesis*, says,

> "Come, hospitable Zeus, with lofty head."

Another poet speaks of Pericles as sitting

> Bowed down with a dreadful frown,
> Because matters of state have gone wrong,
> Until at last, from his head so vast,
> His ideas burst forth in a throng.

Most writers tell us that his tutor in music was **Damon**, who, it seems, was a **Sophist** of the highest order, who used the name of music to conceal this accomplishment from the world, but who really trained Pericles for his political contests just as a trainer prepares an athlete for the games.

Pericles also attended the lectures of **Zeno** of Elea on natural philosophy, in which that philosopher followed the method of **Parmenides**. Zeno moreover had made a special study of how to reduce any man to silence who questioned him, and how to enclose him between the horns of a dilemma.

Pericles /PEHR-uh-kleez/ was a Greek citizen and statesman who lived c. 495-429 BCE.

Akamantis /ahk-uh-MAN-tis/ was one of the tribes, or clans, of ancient Greece. It was named for the Greek hero Acamas /ah-KA-mus/, the son of Theseus. He fought in the Trojan War and was one of the soldiers who stowed away inside the Trojan Horse.

Xanthippus /zan-THĬ-pus/ (c. 525-475 BCE) was Pericles' father and fought in the famous battles of Marathon, Salamis, and **Mykale** /MĬ-kuh-lee/ in which the Greek city-states of Athens, Sparta, and Corinth banded together to fight the Persian King Xerxes I in 479 BCE.

CMPLENARY.COM You can see a marble bust of Pericles wearing his **helmet** on the CMP website.

Plutarch Picture Study See Print #2 in the Plutarch Picture Study for Pericles.

Damon /DĀ-mun/ was a Greek musician who taught Pericles music as well as politics by employing the **Sophist** methods of philosophy and rhetoric.

Parmenides /par-MĬN-uh-deez/ was a Greek philosopher who taught that all of nature is timeless, uniform, necessary, and unchanging. **Zeno** was a student of Parmenides.

Anaxagoras /uh-năk-SĂG-uh-rus/ (510-428 BCE) was a Greek scientist and philosopher. He gave scientific reasons for natural phenomena. He correctly explained the reason for eclipses, and he claimed the sun was a fiery mass, both of which directly opposed the traditional Greek view that these phenomena were caused by the gods.

Sublimity (noun) – the quality of being sublime: to elevate or exalt especially in dignity or honor; to render finer, as in purity or excellence

Buffoonery (noun) – behavior that is ridiculous but amusing

Imperturbable (adj) – unable to be upset or excited; calm

Lampon was a soothsayer and interpreter of oracles.

But it was **Anaxagoras** who had most to do with forming Pericles's style, teaching him an elevation and **sublimity** of expression beyond that of ordinary popular speakers, and altogether purifying and ennobling his mind. This Anaxagoras was called *Nous*, or Intelligence, by the men of that day, either because they admired his own intellect, or because he taught that an abstract intelligence is to be traced in all the concrete forms of matter, and that to this, and not to chance, the universe owes its origin.

Pericles greatly admired Anaxagoras, and became deeply interested in these grand speculations, which gave him a haughty spirit and a lofty style of oratory far removed from vulgarity and low **buffoonery**, and also an **imperturbable** gravity of countenance, and a calmness of demeanor and appearance which no incident could disturb as he was speaking, while the tone of his voice never showed that he heeded any interruption. These advantages greatly impressed the people. Once he sat quietly all day in the marketplace dispatching some pressing business, all the while reviled in the foulest terms by some low worthless fellow. Towards evening he walked home, the man following him and heaping abuse upon him. When about to enter his own door, as it was dark, he ordered one of his servants to take a torch and light the man home.

These were not the only advantages which Pericles gained from his intimacy with Anaxagoras, but he seems to have learned to despise those superstitious fears which the common phenomena of the heavens produce in those who, ignorant of their cause, and knowing nothing about them, refer them all to the immediate action of the gods. Knowledge of physical science, while it puts an end to superstitious terrors, replaces them by a sound basis of piety. It is said that once a ram with one horn was sent from the country as a present to Pericles, and that **Lampon** the prophet, as soon as he saw this strong horn growing out of the middle of the creature's forehead, said that as there were two parties in the state, that of **Thucydides** and that of Pericles, he who possessed this mystic animal would unite the two into one. Anaxagoras cut open the beast's skull and pointed out that its brain did not fill the whole space, but was sunken into the shape of an egg, and all collected at that part from which the horn grew.

This **Thucydides** /thoo-SĬD-ĭh-deez/ is the leader of the Conservative party in Athens and Pericles' rival.

There is also an ancient Greek historian of the same name. Both men are mentioned again later in the text.

There is, I imagine, no reason why both the prophet and the natural philosopher should not have been right, the one discovering the cause, and the other the meaning. The one considered why the horn grew so, and for what reason; the other declared what it *meant* by growing so, and for what *end* it took place. Those who say that when the cause of a **portent** is found out the portent is explained away, do not reflect that the same reasoning which explains away heavenly portents would also put an end to the meaning of the conventional signals used by mankind. The ringing of bells, the blaze of beacon fires, and the shadows on a dial are all of them produced by natural causes but have a further meaning. But perhaps all this belongs to another subject.

Portent (noun) – a sign or warning that something, especially something momentous or calamitous, is likely to happen.

Plenary Discussion Questions

1. Why did Greek poets call Pericles a "squill-head"? View the bust of Pericles on The Plenary website.
2. Describe Pericles' style of oratory.
3. Pericles learned debate, politics, and philosophy from Anaxagoras. What are some of his main ideas? Do you agree with those ideas? Why or why not?
4. What do you think of the story of the ram with only one horn? What do you think this story foretells? Why?
5. Discuss the last paragraph. How can scientific reasoning "explain away heavenly portents," and yet those heavenly portents still maintain a "further meaning" for mankind?

Lesson 4
Pericles the Orator

Lesson 4

Pericles the Orator

Pericles when young greatly feared the people. He had a certain personal likeness to the **despot Pisistratus**; and as his own voice was sweet, and he was ready and fluent in speech, old men who had known Peisistratus were struck by his resemblance to him. He was also rich, of noble birth, and had powerful friends, so that he feared he might be banished by **ostracism**, and consequently held aloof from politics, but proved himself a brave and daring soldier in the wars. Pericles engaged in public affairs, taking the popular side, that of the poor and many against that of the rich and few, quite contrary to his own feelings, which were entirely aristocratic. He feared, it seems, that he might be suspected of a design to make himself despot and seeing that **Cimon** took the side of the nobility, and was much beloved by them, he betook himself to the people, as a means of obtaining safety for himself, and a strong party to combat that of Cimon.

Pisistratus /pī-SIS-truh-tus/ was a tyrant who ruled Athens from 561-527 BCE After his death, his sons Hipparchus and Hippias also ruled as tyrants from 527-510 BCE.

Despot (noun) – a ruler or other person who holds absolute power, typically one who exercises it in a cruel or oppressive way

Ostracism (noun) – temporary banishment from a city by popular vote

Cimon /SĪ-mun/ was a Greek statesman and general who lived from 510-450 BCE. He also led the Athenian aristocratic party against Pericles. Cimon is also the subject of one of Plutarch's *Lives*.

He immediately altered his mode of life; was never seen in any street except that which led to the marketplace and the national assembly and declined all invitations to dinner and social gatherings so utterly that during the whole of his long political life he never dined with one of his friends except when his first cousin was married. On this occasion he sat at the table till the **libations** were poured, upon which he at once got up and went away. For **solemnity** is **wont** to unbend at festive gatherings. True virtue, indeed, appears more glorious the more it is seen, and a really good man's life is never so much admired by the outside world as by his own intimate friends.

Libation (noun) – a drink poured out as an offering to a god

Solemnity (noun) – the state of being serious and dignified

Wont (adj) – inclined to

Wishing to adopt a style of speaking **consonant** with his **haughty** manner and lofty spirit, Pericles made free use of the instrument which Anaxagoras put into his hand and often tinged his oratory

Consonant (adj) – in harmony with

Haughty (adj) – arrogantly superior

Consummation (noun) – the point at which something is complete or finalized

Plato /PLĀ-tō/ (c. 428-348 BCE) was a Greek philosopher who founded the Academy at Athens. He is one of the world's best known and most widely read philosophers. His most famous writings include his *Dialogues*, *Apology*, and *The Republic*. He was a student of Socrates and one of his most famous students was Aristotle.

This **Thucydides** /thoo-SĬD-ĭh-deez/ is the leader of the Conservative party in Athens and Pericles' rival.

Tribune (noun) – a raised platform from which an assembly is addressed

Peloponnesus (noun) – a peninsula in the Southern part of Greece forming the early Mycenean civilization and the powerful city-states of Sparta, Argos, Olympia, and Corinth.

with natural philosophy. He far surpassed all others by using this "lofty intelligence and power of universal **consummation**," as the divine **Plato** calls it; in addition to his natural advantages, adorning his oratory with apt illustrations drawn from physical science.

For this reason, some think that he was nicknamed the Olympian. The comedies of that time, when they allude to him, either in jest or earnest, always appear to think that this name was given him because of his manner of speaking, as they speak of him as "thundering and lightening," and "rolling fateful thunders from his tongue." A saying of **Thucydides** has been preserved, which jestingly testifies to the power of Pericles's eloquence. Thucydides was the leader of the conservative party, and for a long time struggled to hold his own against Pericles in debate. One day Archidamus, the King of Sparta, asked him whether he or Pericles was the best wrestler. "When I throw him in wrestling," Thucydides answered, "he beats me by proving that he never was down, and making the spectators believe him."

For all this, Pericles was very cautious about his words, and whenever he ascended the **tribune** to speak, used first to pray to the gods that nothing unfitted for the present occasion might fall from his lips. He left no writings, except the measures which he brought forward, and very few of his sayings are recorded. One of these was that "he saw war coming upon Athens from **Peloponnesus**."

The nobles perceived that Pericles was the most important man in the State, and far more powerful than any other citizen; wherefore, as they still hoped to check his authority, and not allow him to be omnipotent, they set up Thucydides as his rival, a man of good sense but less of a warrior and more of a politician, who, by watching his opportunities, and opposing Pericles in debate, soon brought about a balance of power. He did not allow the nobles to mix themselves up with the people in the public assembly, as they had been wont to do, so that their dignity was lost among the masses; but he collected them into a separate body, and by thus concentrating their strength was able to use it to counterbalance that of the other party. From the beginning these two factions had been but imperfectly welded together, because their tendencies were different; but now the struggle for power between Pericles and Thucydides drew a sharp line of demarcation between them, and one was called the party of the Many, the other that of the Few. Pericles now courted the people in every way, constantly arranging public spectacles, festivals, and processions in the city, by which he educated the Athenians to take pleasure in refined amusements; and also he sent out [ships] in which many of the people served, learning and practicing seamanship. Besides this he sent settlers to [various nearby cities]. By this means he relieved the state of numerous idle agitators, assisted the **necessitous**, and overawed the allies of Athens by placing his colonists near them to watch their behavior.

Necessitous (adj) – lacking the necessities of life; the needy or poor

Plenary Discussion Questions

1. Why did Pericles take "the popular side, that of the poor and many . . . contrary to his own feelings, which were entirely aristocratic"?
2. Why did the nobles want to "check his authority"? How did they do this?
3. What did Pericles do to win over the people?

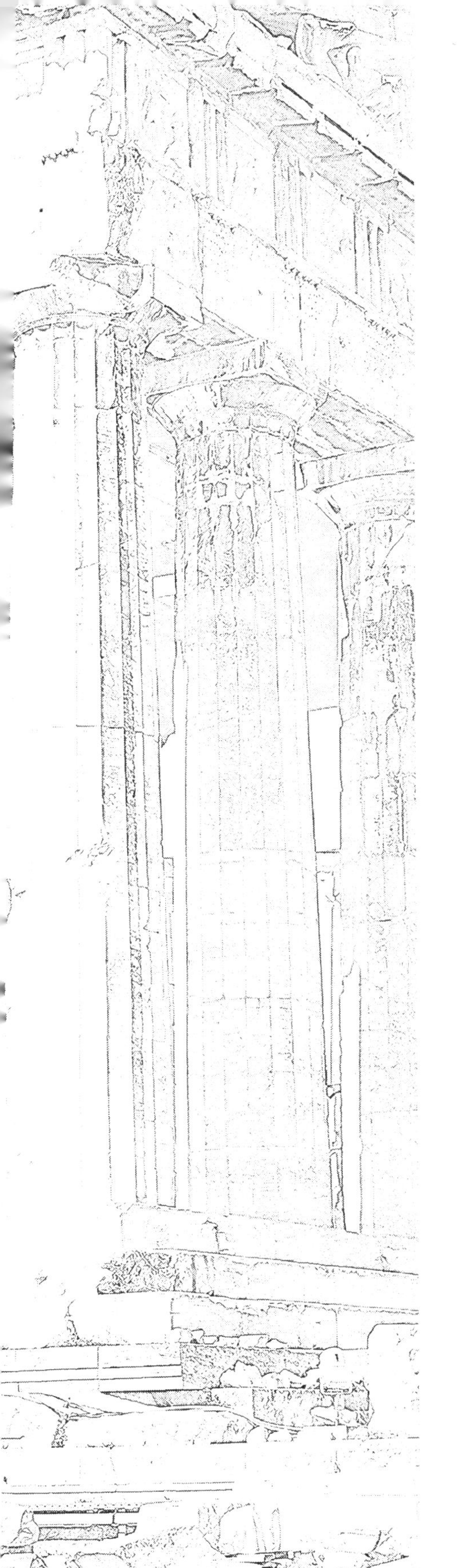

Lesson 5
The Great Buildings of Athens

Lesson 5

The Great Buildings of Athens

The building of the temples, by which Athens was adorned, the people delighted, and the rest of the world astonished, and which now alone prove that the tales of the ancient power and glory of Greece are no fables, was what particularly excited the **spleen** of the opposite faction, who **inveighed** against Pericles in the public assembly, declaring that the Athenians had disgraced themselves. "Greece has been outraged, and feels itself openly tyrannized over, when it sees us using the funds which we extorted from it for the **war against the Persians**, for gilding and beautifying our city, as if it were a vain woman, and adorning it with precious marbles, and statues, and temples worth a thousand **talents**."

Spleen (noun) – bad temper; spite

Inveigh (verb) – to speak or write about something with great hostility

Did You Know? Certain Greek city-states called the *Delian League* banded together in 478 BCE to defend themselves in a **war against the Persian Empire**. It was named after the Island of Delos where the original Congresses were held and the Treasury was kept in the temple of Apollo until Pericles moved it to Athens. All members of the Delian League paid a tax to the joint Treasury.

An Athenian ***talent*** was a measurement of money in Ancient Greece. One talent was equal to 57 lbs. of pure silver.

To this Pericles replied, that the allies had no right to consider how their money was spent, so long as Athens defended them from the Persians; while they supplied neither horses, ships, nor men, but merely money, which the Athenians had a right to spend as they pleased, provided they afforded them that security which it purchased. It was right, he argued, that, after the city had provided all that was necessary for war, it should devote its surplus money to buildings which would be a glory to it for all ages, while these works would create plenty by leaving no man unemployed, and encouraging all sorts of handicraft, so that nearly the whole city would earn wages, and thus derive both its beauty and its profit from itself.

For those who were in the flower of their age, military service offered a means of earning money; while he had laid the foundations of great **edifices** which would require industries of every kind to complete them; and he had done this in the interests of the lower classes, who, although they remained at home, would

Edifice (noun) – a building, especially a large, imposing one

have just as good a claim to their share of the public funds as those who were serving at sea, in garrison, or in the field.

The different materials used, such as stone, brass, ivory, gold, ebony, cypress-wood, and so forth, would require special artisans for each, such as carpenters, modelers, smiths, stonemasons, dyers, molders of gold, ivory painters, embroiderers, workers in **relief**; and also men to bring them to the city, such as sailors and captains of ships for such as came by sea; and, for those who came by land, carriage builders, horse breeders, drivers, rope makers, linen manufacturers, shoemakers, road menders, and miners. Each trade, moreover, employed a number of unskilled laborers, so that, in a word, there would be work for persons of every age and every class, and general prosperity would be the result.

Relief is a sculptural technique where the sculpted elements give the impression that the sculpted material has been raised above the background.

These buildings were of immense size, and unequalled in beauty and grace, as the workmen endeavored to make the execution surpass the design in beauty; but what was most remarkable was the speed with which they were built. All these edifices, each of which one would have thought, it would have taken many generations to complete, were all finished during the most brilliant period of one man's administration. And this makes Pericles' work all the more wonderful, because it was built in a short time, and yet has lasted for ages. In beauty each of them at once appeared **venerable** as soon as it was built; but even at the **present day** the work looks as fresh as ever, for they bloom with an eternal freshness which defies time.

Venerable (adj) – greatly respected due to age, wisdom, or character

Plenary Reminder: At the time of Plutarch's writing, **present day** was c. 110-120 CE.

The overseer and manager of the whole was **Phidias**, although there were other excellent architects and workmen, such as **Callicrates** and **Ictinus**, who built the **Parthenon**. As to the **long wall**, about which **Socrates** says that he heard Pericles bring forward a motion, Callicrates undertook to build it. **Cratinus** satirises the work for being slowly accomplished, saying "He builds in speeches, but he does no work."

Phidias was a Greek sculptor and architect. He oversaw the work done by co-architects **Callicrates** /Kuh-LĬK-ruh-teez/ and **Ictinus** /ĭk-TĪN-us/ as they built the **Parthenon**. Phidias also carved the frieze relief inside the Parthenon.

The **long wall** connected the city of Athens to its seaport at Piraeus.

Socrates /sŏk-ră-teez/ was a Greek philosopher known as the founder of Western philosophy.

Cratinus was a Greek writer of comedic plays.

The **Odeum**, which internally consisted of many rows of seats and many columns, and externally of a roof sloping on all sides

An **Odeum** /Ō-dee-um/ is a building meant for musical and theatrical performances.

from a central point, was said to have been built in imitation of the king of Persia's tent, and was built under Pericles's direction. Pericles at that period used his influence to pass a decree for establishing a musical competition at the **Panathenaic festival**; and, being himself chosen judge, he laid down rules as to how the candidates were to sing and play the flute or the harp. At that period, and ever afterwards, all musical contests took place in the Odeum.

The **Propylaea**, before the **Acropolis**, were finished in five years. A miraculous incident during the work seemed to show that the goddess encouraged and assisted the building. The most energetic and active of the workmen fell from a great height, and lay in a dangerous condition, given over by his doctors. Pericles grieved much for him; but the goddess appeared to him in a dream and suggested a course of treatment by which Pericles quickly healed the workman.

In consequence of this, he set up the brazen statue of ***Athena [Parthenos]***. The golden statue of the goddess was made by Phidias, and his name appears upon the basement in the inscription. Almost everything was in his hands, and he gave his orders to all the workmen – as we have said before – because of his friendship with Pericles. This led to their both being envied; for it was said that Pericles carried on intrigues with Athenian ladies who came ostensibly to see the works. But indeed, how can we wonder at [people] bringing foul accusations against their betters and offering them up as victims to the spite of the populace. So hard is it to discover the truth, because the history of past ages is rendered difficult by the lapse of time; while in contemporary history the truth is always obscured, either by private spite and hatred, or by a desire to curry favor with the chief men of the time.

The **Panathenaic festival** was the greatest festival of Athens. The festival took place every four years and included athletic and musical contests. During the festival, a procession of Athenians made their way to the temple to give sacrifices to Athena.

The **Propylaea** /prŏp-ĭ-LĪ-uh/ was the entrance to the Acropolis.

The **Acropolis** is located atop a hill. It is where many ancient Greek temples and other significant buildings were located. The word *acropolis* is from the Greek word *akron*, which means "highest point," and *polis*, the Greek word for "city."

The ***Athena Parthenos*** was a 37-ft. tall statue that and stood inside the Parthenon. It was made of ivory and gold. *Athena Promachos* was a bronze statue approximately 30-ft. tall that stood outdoors in the middle of the Acropolis as a beacon that could be seen from miles away. Both were built by Phidias.

CMPLENARY.COM You can see several images related to this lesson on the CMP website.

PLUTARCH PICTURE STUDY See Prints #3, #4, and #5 in the Plutarch Picture Study for Pericles.

PLENARY DISCUSSION QUESTIONS

1. CM Exam Question: "In what ways did Pericles make Athens beautiful? How did he persuade the people to help him?"
2. View the paintings and images of the Acropolis, the Parthenon, and the statues of Athena on the CMP website or in the Picture Study for

Pericles. What do you think of Pericles' building project? How would you describe the buildings?

3. Regarding the funds for the war against the Persian Empire, do you think Pericles was right to use the money for his building projects? Why or why not?
4. The Parthenon alone was said to have cost 1,000 Athenian talents. A talent was equal to 57 lbs. of pure silver. Look up the price of silver and calculate how much money that would be today.
5. Compare and contrast the images and descriptions of the two statues of Athena by Phidias: the *Athena Parthenos* and the *Athena Promachos*. Which one do you think was grander?
6. Re-read the last sentence of this lesson. Do you think this sentiment of bias is true? Why or why not? How does a bias of how history is reported affect the way we view it?
7. So far, what do you think about Pericles? Quote any text that supports your answer.

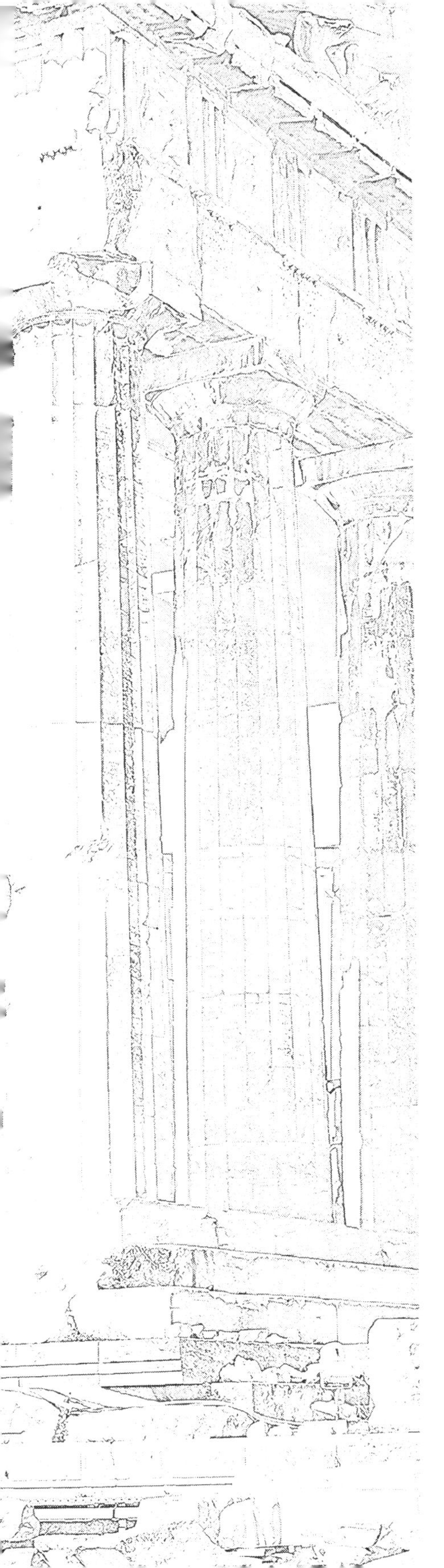

Lesson 6
Pericles Takes Over

Lesson 6

Pericles Takes Over

When the speakers of Thucydides' party complained that Pericles had wasted the public money, and destroyed the revenue, he asked the people in the assembly whether they thought he had spent much. When they answered, "Very much indeed," he said in reply, "Do not, then, put it down to the public account, but to mine; and I will inscribe my name upon all the public buildings." When Pericles said this, the people, either in admiration of his magnificence of manner, or being eager to bear their share in the glory of the new buildings, shouted to him with one accord to take what money he pleased from the treasury, and spend it as he pleased, without stint. And finally, he underwent the **trial of ostracism** with **Thucydides**, and not only succeeded in driving him into exile, but broke up his party.

A **trial of ostracism** in ancient Athens comes from the Greek word *ostraca,* which refers to the broken pieces of pottery that were used as voting tokens. The citizens would cast their votes by having a scribe write the name of the person they thought should be ostracized on a piece of broken pottery. The person who got the most votes would then be banished from the city for 10 years.

CMPLENARY.COM You can see several images of ancient ostraca pottery from Greece on the CMP website.

Thucydides, son of Melesius, was the leader of the Conservative party in Athens and was Pericles' rival. He was banished in c. 442 BCE.

Thucydides the historian was also banished in c. 424 BCE. The two men may have been related.

As now there was no opposition to encounter in the city, and all parties had been blended into one, Pericles undertook the sole administration of the home and foreign affairs of Athens, dealing with the public revenue, the army, the navy, the islands and maritime affairs, and the great sources of strength which Athens derived from her alliances, as well with Greek as with foreign princes and states. Henceforth he became quite a different man: he no longer gave way to the people and ceased to watch the breath of popular favor; but he changed the loose and **licentious** democracy, which had hitherto existed, into a stricter aristocratic, or rather monarchical, form of government.

Licentious (adj) – disregarding accepted rules; lacking legal or moral restraints

This he used honorably and unswervingly for the public benefit, finding the people, as a rule, willing to second the measures which he explained to them to be necessary, and to which he asked their consent, but occasionally having to use violence, and to force them, much against their will, to do what was expedient; like a

Salutary (adj) – beneficial; healthy

Draught (noun) – a serving of a drink; pronounced *draft*

physician dealing with some complicated disorder, who at one time allows his patient innocent recreation, and at another inflicts upon him sharp pains and bitter, though **salutary**, **draughts**.

Every possible kind of disorder was to be found among a people possessing so great an empire as the Athenians; and he alone was able to bring them into harmony, by playing alternately upon their hopes and fears, checking them when over-confident, and raising their spirits when they were cast down and disheartened. Thus, as Plato says, he was able to prove that **oratory** is the art of influencing men's minds, and to use it in its highest application, when it deals with men's passions and characters, which, like certain strings of a musical instrument, require a skillful and delicate touch. The secret of his power is to be found, however, as Thucydides says, not so much in his mere oratory, as in his pure and blameless life, because he was so well known to be incorruptible, and indifferent to money; for though he made the city, into the greatest and richest city of Greece, and though he himself became more powerful than many independent sovereigns who were able to leave their kingdoms to their sons, yet Pericles did not increase by one single **drachma** the estate which he received from his father.

Oratory (noun) – skillful and effective public speaking

A **drachma** is an ancient Greek coin made of silver with a weight of approximately 4.3 grams. The average pay for an Athenian worker during Pericles' time was one drachma per day.

This is the clear account of his power which is given by Thucydides the historian; though the comic poets misrepresent him atrociously, calling his immediate followers the New Peisistratidae, and calling upon him to swear that he never would make himself despot, as though his pre-eminence was not to be borne in a free state. And Telekleides says, that the Athenians delivered up into his hands

> The tribute from the towns, the towns themselves,
> The city walls, to build or to destroy,
> The right of making either peace or war,
> And all the wealth and produce of the land.

And all this was not on any special occasion, or when his administration was especially popular, but for forty years he held the first place among such men as Cimon and Thucydides; and, after the fall and banishment of Thucydides by ostracism, he united in himself for five-and-twenty years all the various offices of state, which were supposed to last only for one year; and yet during the whole of that period proved himself incorruptible by bribes.

As to his paternal estate, he was loth to lose it, and still more to be troubled with the management of it; consequently, he adopted what seemed to him the simplest and most exact method of dealing with it. Every year's produce was sold all together, and with the money thus obtained, he would buy what was necessary for his household in the market, and thus regulate his expenditure. This did not make him popular with his sons when they grew up; nor yet did the women of his family think him a liberal manager, but blamed his exact regulation of his daily expenses, which allowed none of the superfluities common in great and wealthy households, but which made the debit and credit exactly balance each other. These proceedings differed greatly from those of Anaxagoras the philosopher, who left his house, and let his estate go to ruin, while he pursued his lofty speculations.

I conceive, however, that the life of a philosopher and that of a practical politician are not the same, as the one directs his thoughts to abstract ideas, while the other devotes his genius to supplying the real wants of mankind, and in some cases finds wealth not only necessary, but most valuable to him, as indeed it was to Pericles, who assisted many of the poorer citizens. It is said that, as Pericles was engaged in public affairs, Anaxagoras, who was now an old man and in want, covered his head with his robe, and determined to starve himself to death; but when Pericles heard of this, he at once ran to him, and besought him to live, lamenting, not Anaxagoras' fate, but his own, if he should lose so valuable a political adviser. Then Anaxagoras uncovered his head, and said to him, "Pericles, those who want to use a lamp, supply it with oil."

CMPLENARY.COM You can view a painting depicting this encounter between Pericles and Anaxagoras on the CMP website.

Plutarch Picture Study See Print #6 in the Plutarch Picture Study for Pericles.

Plenary Discussion Questions

1. Consider the ancient Greek's use of a "trial of ostracism." Do you think it was a good tool to use? Why or why not? What would happen if we used ostracism in our present-day government?
2. How did Pericles change as a person after he had no opposition?
3. Why do you think Pericles used force "to do what was expedient; like a physician dealing with some complicated disorder"? Is there any example in which you think a government is correct in the use of force against it's own citizenry?
4. What do you think Anaxagoras meant when he said, "Those who want to use a lamp supply it with oil"?

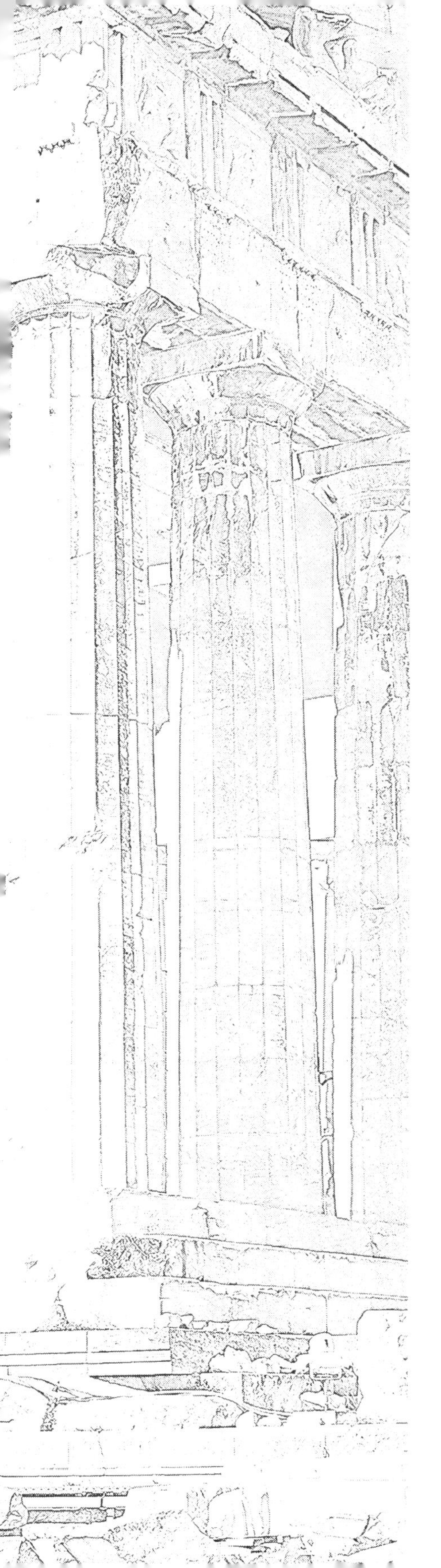

Lesson 7
The First Peloponnesian War

LESSON 7

THE FIRST PELOPONNESIAN WAR

In his campaigns he was chiefly remarkable for caution, for he would not, if he could help it, begin a battle of which the issue was doubtful; nor did he wish to emulate those generals who have won themselves a great reputation by running risks, and trusting to good luck. But he ever used to say to his countrymen, that none of them should come by their deaths through any act of his. Observing that **Tolmides**, elated by previous successes and by the credit which he had gained as a general, was about to invade **Boeotia** in a reckless manner, and had persuaded a thousand young men to follow him without any support whatever, he endeavored to stop him, and made that memorable saying in the public assembly, that if Tolmides would not take the advice of Pericles, he would at any rate do well to consult that best of advisers, Time. This speech had but little success at the time; but when, a few days afterwards, the news came that Tolmides had fallen in action at **Coronea**, and many noble citizens with him, Pericles was greatly respected and admired as a wise and patriotic man.

His most successful campaign was that in the **[Thracian] Chersonese** which proved the salvation of the Greeks residing there: for he not only settled a thousand colonists there, and thus increased the available force of the cities, but built a continuous line of fortifications reaching across the isthmus from one sea to the other, by which he shut off the Thracians, who had previously ravaged the peninsula, and put an end to a constant and harassing border warfare to which the settlers were exposed, as they had for neighbors tribes of wild plundering barbarians.

The First Peloponnesian War was from c. 460-445 BCE. The Second Peloponnesian War began in 431 BCE. Pericles was instrumental in both wars.

Tolmides /TŌL-mīds/ was a leading Athenian General in the Peloponnesian War.

Boeotia /bē-Ō-shē-uh/ is a region in central Greece, just northwest of Athens. Its largest city is Thebes. The Battle of **Coronea** took place in 447 BCE.

The Gallipoli Peninsula in modern day Turkey was known as the **Thracian Chersonese** in the time of Pericles. See map.

CMPLENARY.COM You can see a color **map** of Greece and the surrounding areas that were involved in the Peloponnesian War on the CMP website. A black and white map is also provided in the Appendix.

PLUTARCH PICTURE STUDY See Prints #7 and #8 in the Plutarch Picture Study for Pericles.

But that by which he obtained most glory and renown was when he started from **Pegae in Megara** and sailed round the **Peloponnesus** with a fleet of a hundred **triremes**; for he not only laid waste much of the country near the coast, but he proceeded far inland, away from his ships, leading the troops who were on board, and terrified the inhabitants so much that they shut themselves up in their strongholds. The men of **Sicyon** alone ventured to meet him at **Nemea**, and them he overthrew in a pitched battle, and erected a trophy. And after ravaging the country returned home, having made himself a terror to his enemies, and done good service to Athens; for not the least casualty, even by accident, befell the troops under his command.

When he sailed into the Black Sea with a great and splendidly equipped fleet, he assisted the Greek cities there, and treated them with consideration; and showed the neighboring savage tribes and their chiefs the greatness of his force, and his confidence in his power, by sailing where he pleased, and taking complete control over that sea. He left at **Sinop** thirteen ships, and a land force under the command of **Lamachus**, to act against Timesileon, who had made himself despot of that city. When he and his party were driven out, Pericles passed a decree that six hundred Athenian volunteers should sail to Sinop, and become citizens there, receiving the houses and lands which had formerly been in the possession of the despot and his party. But in other cases he would not agree to the impulsive proposals of the Athenians, and he opposed them when, elated by their power and good fortune, they talked of recovering Egypt and attacking the seaboard of the Persian empire.

Pericles, however, restrained these outbursts, and would not allow the people to meddle with foreign states, but used the power of Athens chiefly to preserve and guard her already existing empire, thinking it to be of paramount importance to oppose the **Lacedaemonians**, a task to which he bent all his energies.

Pegae was a port near the city of **Megara** /MEH-gur-uh/. Pericles invaded there in 453 BCE. The cities of **Nemea** /nē-MĒ-uh/ and **Sicyon** /shĭ-SHEE-on/ are near Corinth, Greece. See map.

A **trireme** /trī-REEM/ was a type of ship used by the ancient Greeks and Romans. It gets its name from the design of the ship which had three rows of oars.

cmplenary.com You can view several pictures and videos of triremes on the CMP website.

Sinop /sĭn-ŌP/ is a city in modern day Turkey located on the coast of the Black Sea.

Lamachus was an Athenian general in the Peloponnesian war. The probable date of his expedition to Sinop was c. 438-432 BCE.

A **Lacedaemonian** was a citizen of the region of Laconia /la-kō-NEE-uh/. Its capital city was, and still is, Sparta.

Did You Know? that the word *laconic* comes from the area of Laconia? It refers to a style of speech or writing which uses very few words. Laconians were famous for their blunt and pithy remarks.

An example of laconic speech involved Philip II of Macedon. After invading southern Greece, he sent a message to Sparta saying, "You are advised to submit without further delay, for if I bring my army into your land, I will destroy your farms, slay your people, and raze your city." The Spartans replied with a single word: "If." Neither Philip nor his son Alexander the Great ever attempted to capture Sparta.

Events proved that Pericles was right in confining the Athenian empire to Greece. First of all **Euboea** revolted, and he was obliged to lead an army to subdue that island. Shortly after this, news came that the Megarians had become hostile, and that an army, under the command of **Pleistoanax**, king of the Lacedaemonians, was menacing the frontier of **Attica**. Pericles now in all haste withdrew his troops from Euboea, to meet the invader. He did not venture on an engagement with the numerous and warlike forces of the enemy, although repeatedly invited by them to fight.

Euboea /yew-BŌ-ee-uh/ is a peninsula near the region of **Attica**, Greece. Athens is the capital of the Attica Region.

Pleistoanax /plī-stō-an-AKS/ was a very young king of Sparta who led the attack on Attica himself in 445 BCE.

But, observing that Pleistoanax was a very young man, and entirely under the influence of **Cleandridas**, whom the **Ephors** had sent to act as his tutor and counsellor because of his tender years, he opened secret negotiations with the latter, who at once, for a bribe, agreed to withdraw the Peloponnesians from Attica. When their army returned and dispersed, the Lacedaemonians were so incensed that they imposed a fine on their king, and condemned Cleandridas, who fled the country, to be put to death. This Cleandridas was the father of **Gylippus**, who caused the ruin of the Athenian expedition in Sicily. **Avarice** seems to have been hereditary in the family, for Gylippus himself, after brilliant exploits in war, was convicted of taking bribes, and banished from Sparta in disgrace. This is more fully set forth in the ***Life of Lysander***.

Cleandridas /klee-an-DRĪ-dus/ was a Spartan General under the command of Pleistoanax. Cleandridas' son was **Gylippus** /jĭl-ĬP-us/.

The **Ephors** were 5 elected magistrates in Sparta who shared power with the Spartan kings.

Avarice (noun) – extreme greed for wealth or material gain

The ***Life of Lysander*** is another one of Plutarch's *Lives*.

When Pericles submitted the accounts of the campaign to the people, there was an item of ten talents, "for a necessary purpose," which the people passed without any questioning, or any curiosity to learn the secret. Some historians say that Pericles sent ten talents annually to Sparta, by means of which he bribed the chief magistrates to defer the war, thus not buying peace, but time to make preparations for a better defense. He immediately turned his attention to the insurgents in Euboea, and proceeding thither with a fleet of fifty sail, and five thousand heavy armed troops, he reduced their cities to submission. He banished from

Chalcis the "**equestrian order**," as it was called, consisting of men of wealth and station; and he drove all the inhabitants of **Hestiaea** out of their country, replacing them by Athenian settlers.

He treated these people with this pitiless severity, because they had captured an Athenian ship, and put its crew to the sword.

Chalcis is a town in Euboea. The "equestrian order" were the city's wealthiest citizens.

Hestiaea is also a town in Euboea.

Plenary Discussion Questions

1. What was Pericles known for in his wartime campaigns? Why do you think that is?
2. Study the two maps of the Peloponnesian War (the first map is in the Appendix and the second map is on The Plenary website). Which cities were in the Delian League led by Athens? And which cities were part of the Spartan League?
3. Watch the video about triremes on the CMP website. What made these ships so important in the Peloponnesian War?

Lesson 8
The Second Peloponnesian War

Lesson 8

The Second Peloponnesian War

After this, as the Athenians and Lacedaemonians made a truce for thirty years, Pericles decreed the expedition against **Samos**, on the pretext that they had disregarded the commands of the Athenians, to cease from their war with the **Milesians**. It was thought that he began this war to please **Aspasia**, and this is, therefore, a good opportunity to discuss that person's character, and how she possessed so great influence and ability that the leading politicians of the day were at her feet, while philosophers discussed and admired her discourse. It is agreed that she was of Milesian origin and she is said to have reserved her favors for the most powerful personages in Greece, in imitation of Thargelia, an Ionian lady of ancient times, of great beauty, ability, and attractions, who had many lovers among the Greeks, and brought them all over to the Persian interest, by which means the seeds of the Persian faction were sown in many cities of Greece, as they were all men of great influence and position.

Now some writers say that Pericles valued Aspasia only for her wisdom and political ability. Indeed Socrates and his friends used to frequent her society; and those who listened to her discourse used to bring their wives with them, that they too might profit by it, although her profession was far from being honorable or decent, for she kept **courtesans** in her house. **Aeschines** says that **Lysicles**, a low-born and low-minded man, became one of the first men in Athens because he lived with Aspasia after Pericles's death. In Plato's *Dialogue* too, she was thought to discuss questions of rhetoric with many Athenians. But Pericles seems to have been more enamored of Aspasia's person than her intellect.

The taking of **Samos** /SĀ-mus/ in Ionia (in present day Turkey) ended the truce between Athens and Sparta.

Milesians /mĭ-LEE-zhans/ were citizens of Miletus /MĪ-lee-tus/, an ancient Greek city in modern day Turkey.

Aspasia /ă-SPĀ-zhuh/ (470-400 BCE) was the second wife or partner of Pericles. Their marital status is unknown. She was known and appreciated for her intellect, which attracted many well-known writers and philosophers of Athens, including Socrates. She is mentioned in the writings of Plato, Aristophanes, Xenophon, and Plutarch, of course. These writings provide insight to the understanding of women in ancient Greece.

CMPLENARY.COM You can see several paintings depicting Aspasia on the CMP website.

Plutarch Picture Study See Print #9 in the Plutarch Picture Study for Pericles.

Courtesan (noun) – a prostitute, especially one with wealthy or upper-class clientele

Aeschines Socraticus (c. 425-350 BCE) was a student of Socrates and wrote many Socratic dialogues, including one about Aspasia. **Lysicles** was an Athenian General.

He was married to a woman who was nearly related to him. By her Pericles had two sons, Xanthippus and Paralus; but afterwards, as they could not live comfortably together, he, at his wife's wish, handed her over to another husband, and himself lived with Aspasia, of whom he was passionately fond. It is said that he never went in or out of his house during the day without kissing her. In the comedies of the time, she is spoken of as the new **Omphale** and as **Deianira**, and sometimes as **Hera**. He is thought to have had a bastard son by her, who is mentioned by **Eupolis** in his play of "The Townships," where Pericles is introduced, asking, "Lives then my son?" to which **Myronides** answers:

> He lives, and long had claimed a manly name,
> But that he feared his harlot mother's shame.

These particulars about Aspasia occurred to my memory, and I thought that perhaps I might please my readers by relating them.

Pericles is accused of going to war with Samos to save the Milesians at the request of Aspasia. These States were at war about the possession of the city of **Priéne**, and the Samians, who were victorious, would not lay down their arms and allow the Athenians to settle the matter by arbitration, as they ordered them to do. For this reason, Pericles proceeded to Samos, put an end to the **oligarchical** form of government there, and sent fifty hostages and as many children to **Lemnos**, to ensure the good behavior of the leading men. It is said that each of these hostages offered him a talent for his own freedom, and that much more was offered by that party which was loth to see a democracy established in the city. Besides all this, **Pissuthnes** the Persian, who had a liking for the Samians, sent and offered him ten thousand pieces of gold if he would spare the city. Pericles, however, took none of these bribes, but returned to Athens. The Samians now at once revolted, as Pissuthnes managed to get them back their hostages, and furnished them with the means of carrying on the war. Pericles now made a second expedition against them, and found them in no mind to submit quietly, but determined to dispute the empire

According to Greek mythology, **Deianira** was the wife of Hercules and **Omphale** was his mistress. Omphale was also the Queen of Lydia. According to Greek mythology, Hercules was ordered to be Omphale's servant for at least one year as punishment for killing a man in a fit of rage. Hercules later married Omphale.

Hera, is the Greek goddess of marriage, women, family, and childbirth. She was the wife of Zeus.

Eupolis (446-411 BCE) was a comic playwrite of ancient Greece. The play in which he targets Pericles and Aspasia is called *The Demes* (Long translates it here as *The Townships*). In it, Eupolis mentions **Myronides,** who was an Athenian General in the First Peloponnesian War.

Priéne was an ancient Greek city which was located between Samos and Miletus in modern day Turkey.

Oligarchy (noun) – a small group of people who have total control of a country's government

Lemnos is a Greek island in the Aegean Sea.

Pissuthnes was the governor of Lydia and served under the Persian king Artaxerxes the 1st. He supported the oligarchs of Samos and opposed Athens.

of the seas with the Athenians. Pericles gained a **signal** victory over them in a sea-fight off the **Goats' Island**, beating a fleet of seventy ships with only forty-four, twenty of which were transports.

Simultaneously with his victory and the flight of the enemy he obtained command of the harbor of Samos and besieged the Samians in their city. They, in spite of their defeat, still possessed courage enough to sally out and fight a battle; but soon a larger force arrived from Athens, and the Samians were completely blockaded.

Pericles now with sixty ships sailed into the Mediterranean intending to meet the Phoenician fleet which was coming to help the Samians. Whatever his intention may have been, his expedition was a failure. In the battle the Samians proved victorious, taking many Athenians prisoners, and destroying many of their ships.

Did You Know? According to Greek mythology, the island of Lemnos was inhabited by women who had murdered every man on the island. Their husbands had cheated on them with Thracian women, and, in revenge, the women decided to kill all their male relatives as they slept. The Lemnos women lived without men until Jason and the Argonauts landed on the island during their quest for the Golden Fleece. Jason fell in love with Hypsipyle, the queen of the island. The Argonauts lived with the women of Lemnos for two years and created a new race of people who were known as the Minyans.

Signal (adj) – notable, remarkable

Goats' Island is the current day island of Agathonisi, Greece.

Plenary Discussion Questions

1. What do you think of Aspasia and her relationship with Pericles?
2. A scholar once stated that, "To ask questions about Aspasia's life is to ask questions about half of humanity." How does Plutarch's description of Aspasia help us understand the role of women in ancient Greece?

Lesson 9
Pericles' Funeral Speech

Lesson 9

Pericles' Funeral Speech

When Pericles heard of the disaster which had befallen his army, he returned in all haste to assist them. He beat **Melissus**, who came out to meet him, and, after putting the enemy to **rout**, at once built a wall round their city, preferring to reduce it by blockade to risking the lives of his countrymen in an assault. As time went on the Athenians became impatient and eager to fight, and it was hard to restrain their **ardor**. Pericles divided the whole force into eight divisions and made them all draw lots. The division which drew the white bean he permitted to feast and take their ease, while the rest did their duty. For this reason, those who are enjoying themselves call it a "white day," in allusion to the white bean. **Ephorus** tells us that Pericles made use of battering engines in this siege, being attracted by their novelty.

In the ninth month of the siege the Samians surrendered. Pericles demolished their walls, confiscated their fleet, and imposed a heavy fine upon them, some part of which was paid at once by the Samians, who gave hostages for the payment of the remainder at fixed periods.

Pericles, after the reduction of Samos, returned to Athens, where he buried those who had fallen in the war in a magnificent manner, and was much admired for the **funeral oration** which, as is customary, was spoken by him over the graves of his countrymen. When he descended from the **rostrum** the women greeted him, crowning him with garlands and ribbons like a victorious athlete, and **Elpinice,** drawing near to him said, "A fine exploit, truly, Pericles, and well worthy of a crown, to lose many of our brave fellow-citizens, not fighting with Persians or Phoenicians, as my brother Cimon did, but in ruining a city of men of our own blood

Melissus /muh-LĬ-sus/ of Samos was the commander of the Samian naval fleet.

Rout (verb) – defeat and cause to retreat in disorder

Ardor (noun) – enthusiasm or passion

Ephorus /EH-fer-us/ was an ancient Greek historian.

Pericles' **funeral oration** is one of the most famous speeches of all time. You can read a shortened version of it in the appendix.

cmplenary.com To see a painting of Pericles giving his Funeral Oration, go to the Pericles Resources page on the CMP website.

Plutarch Picture Study See Print #10 in the Plutarch Picture Study for Pericles.

Rostrum (noun) – a raised platform on which a person stands to make a public speech

Elpinice was a noble woman of ancient Greece. She was the daughter of Militiades and half-sister to Cimon.

and our own allies." At these words of Elpinice, Pericles merely smiled and repeated the verse of **Archilochus**—

"Too old thou art for rich perfumes."

Archilochus was an ancient Greek poet.

Plenary Discussion Questions

1. Read Pericles' funeral oration in the Appendix. Make a list of Pericles' main points in his speech.
2. Do you think it deserves to be called one of the most famous speeches in history? Why or why not?
3. Compare and contrast it with Abraham Lincoln's Gettysburg Address. How are the two speeches similar? Do you think Lincoln used Pericles' speech as inspiration?

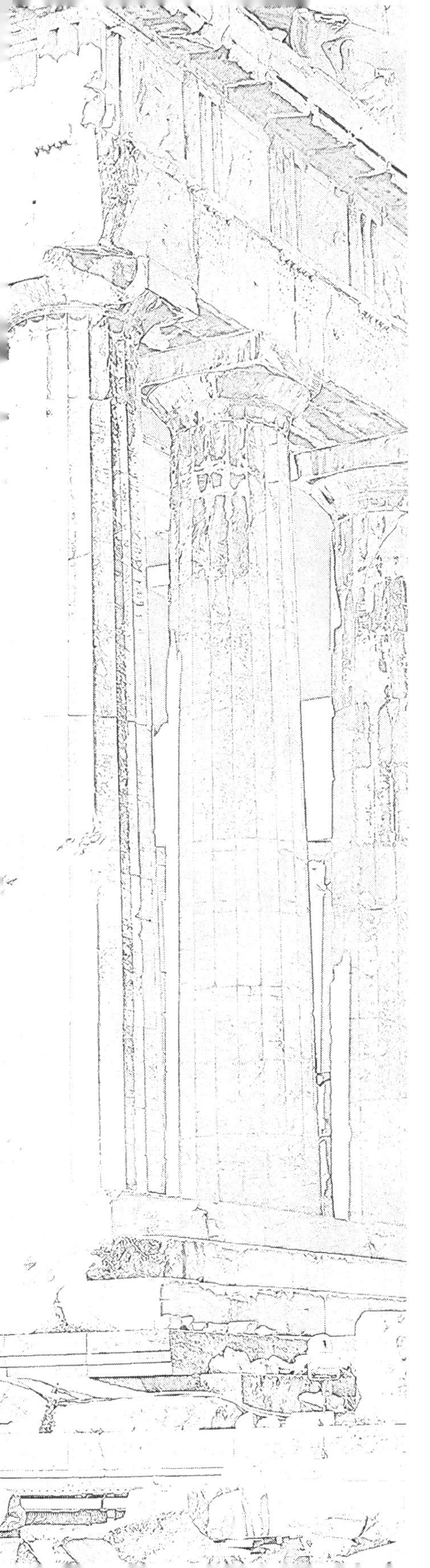

Lesson 10
The Plague

Lesson 10

The Plague

After these events, as the clouds were gathering for the Peloponnesian war, Pericles persuaded the Athenians to send assistance to the people of **Corcyra**, who were at war with the Corinthians, and thus to attach to their own side an island with a powerful naval force, at a moment when the Peloponnesians had all but declared war against them.

Corcyra is now known as the Greek town of Corfu.

When the people passed this decree, Pericles sent only ten ships under the command of **Lacedaemonius**, the son of Cimon, as if he designed a deliberate insult. His design in sending Lacedaemonius out, against his will, and with so few ships, was that if he performed nothing brilliant, he might be accused, even more than he was already, of leaning to the side of the Spartans. Indeed, by all means in his power, he always threw obstacles in the way of the advancement of Cimon's family.

Lacedaemonius was a General in the Athenian army. He was the grandson of the famous General Miltiades IV and the son of the Athenian politician, Cimon, who was Pericles' rival. The name *Lacedaemonius* comes from *Lacedaemon*, which was another name for the city of Sparta.

Now Pericles was much reproached for sending these ten ships, which were of little value to the Corcyreans, and gave a great handle to his enemies to use against him, and in consequence sent a larger force after them to Corcyra, which arrived there after the battle. The Corinthians, enraged at this, complained in the congress of Sparta of the conduct of the Athenians, as did also the Megarians, who said that they were excluded from every market and every harbor which was in Athenian hands, contrary to the ancient rights and common privileges of the **Hellenic** race.

The **Hellenic race** is another name for the people of Greece.

At this time, too, **Potidaea**, a city subject to Athens, but a colony of Corinth, revolted, and its siege materially hastened the outbreak of the war. Archidamus, the king of the Lacedaemonians, sent ambassadors to Athens, was willing to submit all disputed points to arbitration, and endeavored to moderate the excitement of his allies, so that war probably would not have broken out if the

The **Potidaea** /poh-tĭ-DEE-uh/ revolt against Athens took place in 432 BCE.

Athenians could have been persuaded to rescind their decree of exclusion against the Megarians, and to come to terms with them. And, for this reason, Pericles, who was particularly opposed to this, and urged the people not to give way to the Megarians, alone bore the blame of having begun the war.

Acharnae /uh-KAR-nee/ was a suburb located just north of ancient Athens.

The Lacedaemonians invaded Attica with a great host of their own troops and those of their allies, led by Archidamus, their king. They proceeded, ravaging the country as they went, as far as **Acharnae** where they encamped, imagining that the Athenians would never endure to see them there, but would be driven by pride and shame to come out and fight them. However, Pericles thought that it would be a very serious matter to fight for the very existence of Athens against sixty thousand Peloponnesian and Boeotian heavy-armed troops, and so he pacified those who were dissatisfied at his inactivity by pointing out that trees when cut down quickly grow again, but that when the men of a State are lost, it is hard to raise up others to take their place. He would not call an assembly of the people, because he feared that they would force him to act against his better judgment, but, just as the captain of a ship, when a storm comes on at sea, places everything in the best trim to meet it, and trusting to his own skill and seamanship, disregarding the tears and entreaties of the sea-sick and terrified passengers; so did Pericles shut the gates of Athens, place sufficient forces to ensure the safety of the city at all points, and calmly carry out his own policy, taking little heed of the noisy grumblings of the discontented. Many of his friends besought him to attack, many of his enemies threatened him and abused him, and many songs and offensive jests were written about him, speaking of him as a coward, and one who was betraying the city to its enemies.

Pericles sent a fleet of a hundred ships to attack Peloponnesus, but did not sail with it himself, remaining at home to keep a tight hand over Athens until the Peloponnesians drew off their forces. He regained his popularity with the common people, who suffered much from the war, by giving them allowances of money from the public revenue, and grants of land; for he drove out the entire population of the island of Aegina and divided the land by lot among the Athenians. A certain amount of relief also was experienced by reflecting upon the injuries which they were inflicting on the enemy; for the fleet as it sailed round Peloponnesus destroyed many small villages and cities, and ravaged a great extent of country, while Pericles himself led an expedition into the territory of Megara and laid it all waste.

By this it is clear that the allies, although they did much damage to the Athenians, yet suffered equally themselves, and never could have protracted the war for such a length of time as it really lasted, but, as Pericles foretold, must soon have desisted had not Providence interfered and confounded human counsels. For now the pestilence fell among the Athenians, and cut off the flower of their youth. Suffering both in body and mind they raved against Pericles, just as people when delirious with disease attack their fathers or their physicians. They endeavored to ruin him, urged on by his personal enemies, who assured them that he was the author of the **plague**, because he had brought all the country people into the city, where they were compelled to live during the heat of summer, crowded together in small rooms and stifling tents, living an idle life too, and breathing foul air instead of the pure country breezes to which they were accustomed. The cause of this, they said, was the man who, when the war began, admitted the masses of the country people into the city, and then made no use of them, but allowed them to be penned up together like cattle, and transmit the contagion from one to another, without devising any remedy or alleviation of their sufferings.

Hoping to relieve them somewhat, and also to annoy the enemy, Pericles manned a hundred and fifty ships, placed on board, besides the sailors, many brave infantry and cavalry soldiers, and was about to put to sea. The Athenians conceived great hopes, and the enemy no less terror from so large an armament. When all was ready, and Pericles himself had just embarked in his own trireme, an eclipse of the sun took place, producing total darkness,

Did You Know? The **plague** that gripped Athens in 429 BCE killed one-quarter to one-third of the city's population. Scientists now think it might have been Typhus or Smallpox that ravaged the city, not the Bubonic plague. Thucydides describes the horrific symptoms:
"Many who were in perfect health, all in a moment, and without any apparent reason, were seized with violent heats in the head and with redness and inflammation of the eyes. Internally the throat and the tongue were quickly suffused with blood, and the breath became unnatural and fetid . . . in a short time the disorder, accompanied by a violent cough, reached the chest; then fastening lower down, it would move the stomach and bring on all the vomits of bile to which physicians have ever given names . . . The body externally was not so very hot to the touch, nor yet pale; it was of a livid color inclining to red and breaking out in pustules and ulcers." – *History of the Peloponnesian War* by Thucydides (translation by Benjamin Jowett)

Plenary Discussion Questions

1. CM Exam Question: "How did Pericles manage the people in time of war lest they should force him to act against his own judgement?"
2. What is Plutarch saying about Pericles in this quote: "just as the captain of a ship, when a storm comes on at sea, places everything in the best trim to meet it, and trusting to his own skill and seamanship, disregarding the tears and entreaties of the sea-sick and terrified passengers, so did Pericles shut the gates of Athens."
3. Why did the people of Athens vote to condemn Pericles? Were they correct in doing so? Why or why not?

and all men were terrified at so great a portent. Pericles, observing that his helmsman was alarmed and knew not what to do, held his cloak over the man's eyes and asked him if he thought that a terrible portent. As he answered that he did not, Pericles said: "What is the difference, then, between it and an eclipse of the sun, except that the eclipse is caused by something larger than my cloak?" This subject is discussed by the philosophers in their schools.

Pericles sailed with the fleet, but did nothing worthy of so great a force. He besieged the sacred city of Epidaurus, but, although he had great hopes of taking it, he failed on account of the plague, which destroyed not only his own men, but everyone who came in contact with them. After this he again endeavored to encourage the Athenians, to whom he had become an object of dislike. However, he did not succeed in pacifying them, but they condemned him by a public vote to be general no more, and to pay a fine which is stated at the lowest estimate to have been fifteen talents, and at the highest fifty.

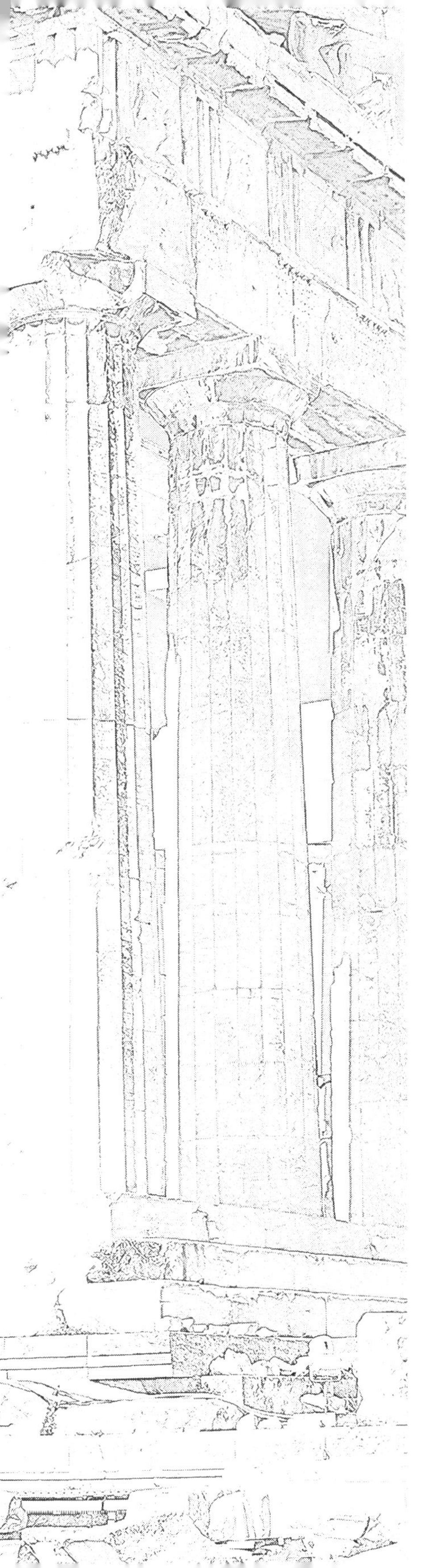

Lesson 11
The Age of Pericles Comes to an End

Lesson 11

The Age of Pericles Comes to an End

He soon regained his public position, for the people's outburst of anger was quenched by the blow they had dealt him, just as a bee leaves its sting in the wound; but his private affairs were in great distress and disorder, as he had lost many of his relatives during the plague, while others were estranged from him on political grounds. **Xanthippus** too, the eldest of his legitimate sons, who was a spendthrift by nature and married to a woman of expensive habits, could not bear with his father's stingy ways and the small amount of money which he allowed him. He consequently sent to one of his friends and borrowed money from him as if Pericles had authorized him to do so. When the friend asked for his money back again, Pericles prosecuted him, at which proceeding young Xanthippus was enraged and abused his father, sneering at his way of life and his discussions with the sophists. Xanthippus put about that scandal about his father and his own wife, so that the father and son remained irreconcilable enemies until Xanthippus's death, which happened during the plague, by an attack of that disorder.

Xanthippus /zan-THĬ-pus/ was the oldest son of Pericles by his first wife.

At the same time Pericles lost his sister and most of his relations, especially those who supported his policy. Yet he would not yield, nor abate his firmness and constancy of spirit because of these afflictions, but was not observed to weep or mourn, or attend the funeral of any of his relations, until he lost Paralus, the last of his legitimate offspring. Crushed by this blow, he tried in vain to keep up his grand air of indifference, and when carrying a garland to lay upon the corpse he was overpowered by his feelings, so as to burst into a passion of tears and sobs, which he had never done before in his whole life.

Athens made trial of her other generals and public men to conduct her affairs, but none appeared to be of sufficient weight or reputation to have such a charge entrusted to him. The city longed for Pericles and invited him again to lead its counsels and direct its armies; and he, although dejected in spirits and living in seclusion in his own house, was yet persuaded by Alcibiades and his other friends to resume the direction of affairs. The people apologized for their ungrateful treatment of him, and when he was again in office and elected as general, he begged of them to be released from the operations of the law of bastardy, which he himself had originally introduced, in order that his name and race might not altogether become extinct for want of an heir.

The provisions of the law were as follows: Pericles many years before, when he was at the height of his power and had children born to him, as we have related, of legitimate birth, proposed a law that only those born of an Athenian father and mother should be reckoned Athenian citizens. But when the king of Egypt sent a present of forty thousand ***medimni*** of wheat to be divided among the citizens, many lawsuits arose about the citizenship of men whose birth had never been questioned before that law came into force, and many vexatious informations were laid. Nearly five thousand men were convicted of illegitimacy of birth and sold for slaves, while those who retained their citizenship and proved themselves to be genuine Athenians amounted to fourteen thousand and forty. It was indeed an unreasonable request that a law which had been enforced in so many instances should now be broken in the person of its own author, but Pericles's domestic misfortunes, in which he seemed to have paid the penalty for his former haughtiness and pride, touched the hearts of the Athenians so much that they thought his sorrows deserving of their pity, and his request such as he was entitled to make and they to grant in common charity, and they consented to his illegitimate son being enrolled in his own tribe and bearing his own name. This [son, **Pericles the Younger**] was subsequently put to death by the

A ***medimni*** was equal to almost 15 bushels.

Pericles' son by Aspasia was also named Pericles and was often referred to as **Pericles the Younger**. He was executed with other naval officers for failing to rescue their own drowning men during the naval battle of Arginusae in 406 BCE.

people, together with all his colleagues, for their conduct after the sea-fight at Arginusae.

After this it appears that Pericles was attacked by the plague, not acutely or continuously, as in most cases, but in a slow wasting fashion, exhibiting many varieties of symptoms, and gradually undermining his strength. **Theophrastus**, in his treatise on Ethics, discusses whether a man's character can be changed by disease, and whether virtue depends upon bodily health. As an example, he quotes a story that Pericles, when one of his friends came to visit him during his sickness, showed him a charm hung round his neck, as a proof that he must be indeed ill to submit to such a piece of folly. As he was now on his deathbed, the most distinguished of the citizens and his surviving friends collected round him and spoke admiringly of his nobleness and immense power, enumerating also the number of his exploits, and the trophies which he had set up for victories gained; for while in chief command he had won no less than nine victories for Athens.

Theophrastus /thee-uh-FRĂS-tus/ was a Greek philosopher who studied under Aristotle.

They were talking thus to one another in his presence, imagining that he could no longer understand them, but had lost his power of attending to them. He, however, was following all that they said, and suddenly broke silence, saying that he was surprised at their remembering and praising him for the exploits which depended entirely upon fortune for their success, and which many other generals had done as well as himself, while they did not mention his greatest and most glorious title to fame. "No Athenian," said he, "ever wore black because of me."

Pericles was to be admired, not only for his gentleness and mildness of spirit, which he preserved through the most violent political crises and outbreaks of personal hatred to himself, but also for his lofty disposition. He himself accounted it his greatest virtue that he never gave way to feelings of envy or hatred, but from his own exalted pinnacle of greatness never regarded any man as so much his enemy that he could never be his friend. This alone, in my opinion, justifies that outrageous nickname of

Plenary Discussion Questions

1. Discuss the relationship between Pericles and his sons. Was Pericles correct in prosecuting Xanthippus? Why or why not?
2. Why did the city ask Pericles to resume his leadership role?
3. What was the "law of bastardy" and why did Pericles want it overturned? Do you think he was correct to ask that it be overturned? Why or why not?
4. Do you think a man's character can be changed by disease? And if so, do you think this was the case with Pericles?
5. Pericles says his greatest achievement was that "No Athenian ever wore black because of me." Do you think this statement is true? Why or why not?
6. Plutarch says "Pericles was to be admired." Do you agree?

his, and gives it a certain propriety; for so serene and impartial a man, utterly uncorrupt though possessed of great power, might naturally be called Olympian.

Events soon made the loss of Pericles felt and regretted by the Athenians. Those who during his lifetime had complained that his power completely threw them into the shade, when after his death they had made trial of other orators and statesmen, were obliged to confess that with all his arrogance no man ever was really more moderate, and that his real mildness in dealing with men was as remarkable as his apparent pride and assumption. His power, which had been so grudged and envied, and called monarchy and despotism, now was proved to have been the saving of the State; such an amount of corrupt dealing and wickedness suddenly broke out in public affairs, which he before had crushed and forced to hide itself, and so prevented its becoming incurable through impunity and license.

Lesson 12
Pericles and Democracy Today

Lesson 12

Pericles and Democracy Today

"Pericles' long tenure as a political leader, more than thirty years, permitted him to aim at goals that went far beyond the immediate concerns that fully occupy most politicians and statesmen. He was one of those rare individuals who do not merely accept the conditions of the world they find but try to shape it to an image in their own minds. He saw the opportunity to create the greatest political community the world had ever known." (Kagan, *Periclean Athens and Modern Democracy*)

Donald Kagan, a renowned professor at Yale University and an expert on Ancient Greece, writes that Pericles had an unparalleled gift for knowing what the state and its citizens could achieve together in an atmosphere of freedom and mutual trust – a democracy.

"In our time democracy is taken for granted, but it is one of the rarest, most delicate, and fragile flowers in the jungle of human experience. It existed for only two centuries in Athens and less than that in a small number of Greek states. When it reappeared in the Western world more than two millennia later, it was broader but shallower . . . modern democracies are also more remote and indirect, less 'political' in the ancient understanding of the term."

"Only in ancient Athens and in the United States so far has democracy lasted for as much as two hundred years. Monarchy and different forms of despotism, on the other hand, have gone on for millennia . . . Optimists may believe that democracy is the inevitable and final form of human society, but the historical record shows that up to now it has been the rare exception."

"The Athenian democracy, Pericles asserts, far from reducing all to a low common level, raises all its citizens to the level of noblemen by asking them to take part in political life and so to control their own destiny." (Kagan)

And Edith Hamilton says that "for a hundred years, Athens was a city where the great spiritual forces that war in men's minds flowed along together in peace; law and freedom, truth and religion, beauty and goodness, the objective and the subjective – there was a truce to their eternal warfare, and the result was . . . balance and clarity. Athenians saw their city as one that had proved beyond all others that the power of the spirit could be stronger than the power of overwhelmingly great physical forces. She was the abode of 'Excellence, much labored for by the sons of men,' said Artistotle . . . So the men of the early Periclean age saw their city. Pericles bade them gaze at her until they were filled with love for her, for her humanity and self-restraint, for her freedom founded in law, for her service to the things of the mind which made her what Pericles called, 'the school of Hellas.'"

"One cannot but wonder what would have happened if the [Delian] league had succeeded and spread to the rest of Greece. What could a united Greece have done? . . . What might not the West have advanced to if Greece, not Rome, had been the leader? . . . But the Athenian league failed, and the reason was that Athens failed. Her position as the head of the league gave her power; and the greed for more power which, Thucydides insists throughout his history, all power creates, overcame her excellence. In a few years she had forgotten the ideals that saved her from Persia, her devotion to freedom, her spirit of self-restraint. She turned the league of free cities into a league of unwilling subjects to herself. Men called her now not the Liberator, but the Tyrant City." (pgs 32-34)

The demise of democracy in Athens began with the death of Pericles in 429 BCE. Sparta and Athens continued the Peloponnesian War, which lasted another twenty-five years. Sparta won and quickly abolished democracy. The government they established became known as the Thirty Tyrants. Then, almost one hundred years later, Philip of Macedonia and his son, Alexander the Great, conquered all of Greece, and, with that, the Athenian model of democracy died.

But, as the historian Thucydides writes, "The kind of events that once took place will, by reason of human nature, take place again."

Plenary Discussion Questions

1. Do you think Thucydides was right when he says events will repeat themselves? Have they? Explain your answer.
2. Where can you find democracy in the world today?
3. What is the difference between a Democracy and a Republic?
4. Define the style of government in the country where you live. Is it a good form of government? Why or why not?

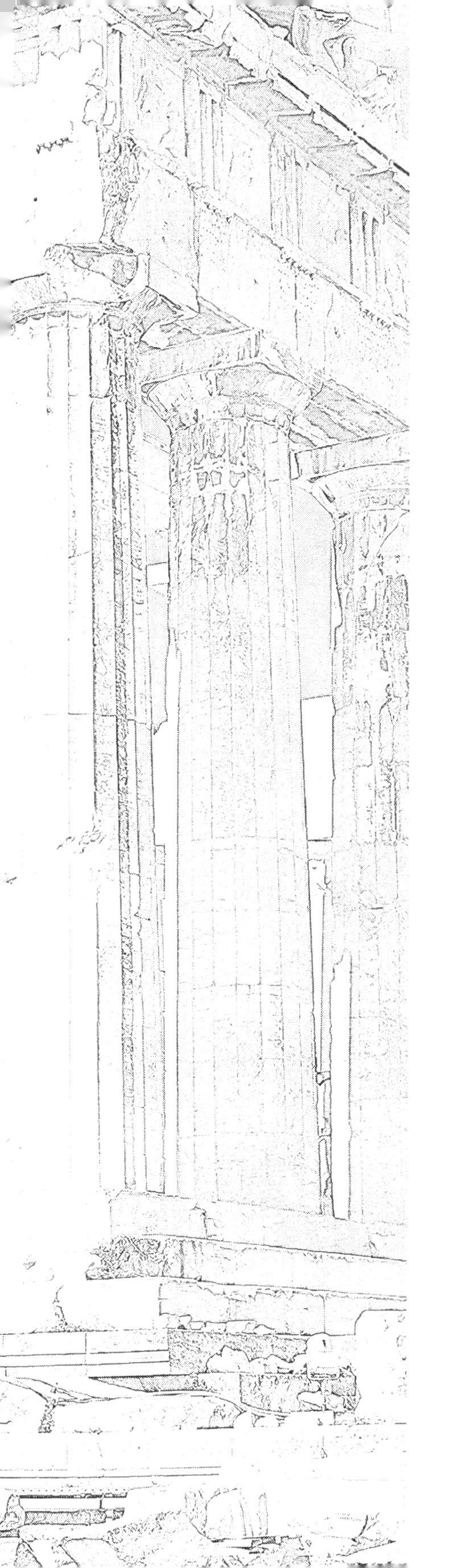

APPENDIX

Map of the Peloponnesian War

FUNERAL ORATION BY PERICLES

INTRODUCTION BY THUCYDIDES

The public sepulcher is situated in the most beautiful spot outside the walls; there they always bury those who fall in war in recognition of their pre-eminent valor. When the remains have been laid in the earth, some man of known ability and high reputation, chosen by the city, delivers a suitable oration over them; after which the people depart. Such is the manner of interment; and the ceremony was repeated from time to time throughout the war. Over those who were the first buried, Pericles was chosen to speak. At the fitting moment he advanced from the sepulcher to a lofty stage, which had been erected in order that he might be heard as far as possible by the multitude, and spoke as follows:

Pericles' funeral oration is recounted by Thucydides in his book, *History of the Peloponnesian War.* Pericles gave the speech in 431 BCE, at the end of the first year of fighting between Athens and Sparta in the Second Peloponnesian War.

It is a masterpiece in rhetoric and is considered to be one of the best speeches ever given. It has been quoted and imitated by other men throughout history. Some historians believe it was the model for Abraham Lincoln's *Gettysburg Address.*

The translation used here is by Benjamin Jowett and has been edited for length.

FUNERAL SPEECH BY PERICLES

I will speak first of our ancestors, for it is right and seemly that now, when we are lamenting the dead, a tribute should be paid to their memory. There has never been a time when they did not inhabit this land, which by their valor they have handed down from generation to generation, and we have received from them a free state. But if they were worthy of praise, still more were our fathers, who added to their inheritance, and after many a struggle transmitted to us their sons this great empire. And we ourselves assembled here today, who are still most of us in the vigor of life, have carried the work of improvement further, and have richly endowed our city with all things, so that she is sufficient for herself both in peace and war. But before I praise the dead, I should like to point out by what principles of action we rose to power, and under what institutions and through what manner of life our empire became great.

Our form of government does not enter into rivalry with the institutions of others. We do not copy our neighbors, but are an example to them. It is true that we are called a democracy, for

CMPLENARY.COM You can see a painting of Pericles delivering his famous Funeral Oration on the CMP website.

PLUTARCH PICTURE STUDY See Print #10 in the Plutarch Picture Study for Pericles.

the administration is in the hands of the many and not of the few. But while the law secures equal justice to all alike in their private disputes, the claim of excellence is also recognized; and when a citizen is in any way distinguished, he is preferred to the public service, not as a matter of privilege, but as the reward of merit. Neither is poverty a bar, but a man may benefit his country whatever be the obscurity of his condition. There is no exclusiveness in our public life, and in our private intercourse we are not suspicious of one another, nor angry with our neighbor if he does what he likes; we do not put on sour looks at him which, though harmless, are not pleasant. A spirit of reverence pervades our public acts; we are prevented from doing wrong by respect for the authorities and for the laws, having an especial regard to those which are ordained for the protection of the injured as well as to those unwritten laws which bring upon the transgressor of them the reprobation of the general sentiment.

And we have not forgotten to provide for our weary spirits many relaxations from toil; we have regular games and sacrifices throughout the year; our homes are beautiful and elegant; and the delight which we daily feel in all these things helps to banish melancholy. Because of the greatness of our city the fruits of the whole earth flow in upon us; so that we enjoy the goods of other countries as freely as of our own.

Then, again, our military training is in many respects superior to that of our adversaries. Our city is thrown open to the world, and we never expel a foreigner or prevent him from seeing or learning anything of which the secret if revealed to an enemy might profit him. We rely not upon management or trickery, but upon our own hearts and hands. And in the matter of education, whereas they from early youth are always undergoing laborious exercises which are to make them brave, we live at ease, and yet are equally ready to face the perils which they face.

If then we prefer to meet danger with a light heart but without laborious training, and with a courage which is gained by habit and not enforced by law, are we not greatly the gainers? Since we do not anticipate the pain, although, when the hour comes, we can be as brave as those who never allow themselves to rest; and thus too, our city is equally admirable in peace and in war.

For we are lovers of the beautiful, yet simple in our tastes, and we cultivate the mind without loss of manliness. Wealth we employ, not for talk and ostentation, but when there is a real use for it. To **avow** poverty with us is no disgrace; the true disgrace is in doing nothing to avoid it. An Athenian citizen does not neglect the state because he takes care of his own household; and even those of us who are engaged in business have a very fair idea of politics. We alone regard a man who takes no interest in public affairs, not as a harmless; but as a useless character; and if few of us are originators, we are all sound judges of a policy. The great impediment to action is, in our opinion, not discussion, but the want of that knowledge which is gained by discussion preparatory to action. For we have a peculiar power of thinking before we act and of acting too, whereas other men are courageous from ignorance but hesitate upon reflection. And they are surely to be esteemed the bravest spirits who, having the clearest sense both of the pains and pleasures of life, do not on that account shrink from danger. In doing good, again, we are unlike others; we make our friends by conferring, not by receiving favors. We alone do good to our neighbors not upon a calculation of interest, but in the confidence of freedom and in a frank and fearless spirit.

Avow (verb) – to declare openly, bluntly, and without shame

And we shall assuredly not be without witnesses; there are mighty monuments of our power which will make us the wonder of this and of succeeding ages; we shall not need the praises of **Homer**, whose poetry may please for the moment, although his representation of the facts will not bear the light of day. For we have compelled every land and every sea to open a path for our valor, and have everywhere planted eternal memorials of our friendship and of our enmity. Such is the city for whose sake these men nobly fought and died; they could not bear the thought that

Homer was an ancient Greek poet who wrote the *Iliad* and the *Odyssey*, two epic poems that are the main works of ancient Greek literature.

she might be taken from them; and every one of us who survive should gladly toil on her behalf.

I have dwelt upon the greatness of Athens because I want to show you that we are contending for a higher prize than those who enjoy none of these privileges, and to establish by manifest proof the merit of these men whom I am now commemorating. Their loftiest praise has been already spoken. For in magnifying the city I have magnified them, and men like them whose virtues made her glorious. And of how few Hellenes can it be said as of them, that their deeds when weighed in the balance have been found equal to their fame! Methinks that a death such as theirs has been given the true measure of a man's worth; it may be the first revelation of his virtues but is at any rate their final seal. For even those who come short in other ways may justly plead the valor with which they have fought for their country; they have blotted out the evil with the good and have benefited the state more by their public services than they have injured her by their private actions.

Enervated (verb) – to weaken

None of these men were **enervated** by wealth or hesitated to resign the pleasures of life; none of them put off the evil day in the hope, natural to poverty, that a man, though poor, may one day become rich. But, deeming that the punishment of their enemies was sweeter than any of these things, and that they could fall in no nobler cause, they determined at the hazard of their lives to be honorably avenged, and to leave the rest. They resigned to hope their unknown chance of happiness; but in the face of death, they resolved to rely upon themselves alone. And when the moment came, they were minded to resist and suffer, rather than to fly and save their lives; they ran away from the word of dishonor, but on the battle-field their feet stood fast, and in an instant, at the height of their fortune, they passed away from the scene, not of their fear, but of their glory.

Such was the end of these men; they were worthy of Athens. I would have you day by day fix your eyes upon the greatness of Athens, until you become filled with the love of her; and when you are impressed by the spectacle of her glory, reflect that this empire has been acquired by men who knew their duty and had the courage to do it, who in the hour of conflict had the fear of dishonor always present to them, and who, if ever they failed in an enterprise, would not allow their virtues to be lost to their country, but freely gave their lives to her as the fairest offering which they could present at her feast. The sacrifice which they collectively made was individually repaid to them; for they received again each one for himself a praise which grows not old. For the whole earth is the sepulcher of famous men; not only are they commemorated by columns and inscriptions in their own country, but in foreign lands there dwells also an unwritten memorial of them, graven not on stone but in the hearts of men.

Wherefore I do not now commiserate the parents of the dead who stand here; I would rather comfort them. You know that your life has been passed amid manifold **vicissitudes**; and that they may be deemed fortunate who have gained most honor, whether an honorable death like theirs, or an honorable sorrow like yours, and whose days have been so ordered that the term of their happiness is likewise the term of their life. I know how hard it is to make you feel this, when the good fortune of others will too often remind you of the gladness which once lightened your hearts. And sorrow is felt at the want of those blessings, not which a man never knew, but which were a part of his life before they were taken from him. Be comforted by the glory of those who are gone. For the love of honor alone is ever young, and not riches, as some say, but honor is the delight of men when they are old and useless.

Vicissitudes (noun) – a change of circumstances or fortune, typically one that is unwelcome or unpleasant

To you who are the sons and brothers of the departed, I see that the struggle to emulate them will be an arduous one. For all men praise the dead, and, however preeminent your virtue may be, hardly will you be thought, I do not say to equal, but even to approach them. The living have their rivals and detractors, but when a man is out of the way, the honor and good-will which he receives is **unalloyed**.

Unalloyed (adj) – complete; pure

I have paid the required tribute, in obedience to the law, making use of such fitting words as I had. The tribute of deeds has been paid in part; for the dead have been honorably interred, and it remains only that their children should be maintained at the public charge until they are grown up: this is the solid prize with which, as with a garland, Athens crowns her sons living and dead, after a struggle like theirs. For where the rewards of virtue are greatest, there the noblest citizens are enlisted in the service of the state. And now, when you have duly lamented, everyone his own dead, you may depart.

Conclusion by Thucydides

Such was the order of the funeral celebrated in this winter, with the end of which ended the first year of the Peloponnesian War.

Bibliography

Asimov, Isaac. *The Greeks: A Great Adventure*. Houghton Mifflin Co., 1965.

Bulfinch, Thomas. *Bulfinch's Mythology*. Grosset & Dunlap, 1883.

Butler, Howard Crosby. *The Story of Athens: A Record of the Life and Art of the City of the Violet Crown Read in Its Ruins and in the Lives of Great Athenians*. The Century Co., 1902.

Hamilton, Edith. *The Echo of Greece*. W.W. Norton and Co., 1957.

—. *The Greek Way*. W.W. Norton and Co., 2017.

Holst, Sanford. *Ancient Athens: Five Intriguing Lives: Socrates, Pericles, Aspasia, Peisistratos and Alcibiades*. Santorini Publishing, 2016.

Kagan, Donald. (1993, June 8). *Periclean Athens and Modern Democracy.* Retrieved from http://www.aei.org/publication/periclean-athens-and-modern-democracy/.

Smith, William. *A Classical Dictionary of Biography, Mythology, and Geography*. John Murray, 1883.

—. *Dictionary of Greek and Roman Antiquities*. John Murray, 1859.

Stewart, Aubrey and George Long. *Plutarch's Lives Translated from the Greek in Four Volumes*. Bell and Sons, 1916.

ABOUT THE AUTHOR

RACHEL LEBOWITZ is the owner of A Charlotte Mason Plenary. She and her husband have always homeschooled their two children using the Charlotte Mason method of education. Rachel currently teaches Shakespeare and Plutarch at a local homeschool co-op and she leads a study group for parents who would like to learn more about implementing Charlotte Mason's methods. She has a Bachelor of Arts degree from the University of Houston where she studied Communications and Political Science. Before attending college, she traveled as a member of *Up With People*, a performing arts organization with a mission to transcend cultural barriers and create global understanding through music. After college, she spent many years as a Radio and Television Journalist. She currently lives in Texas with her husband, two children, two dogs, and one guinea pig.

You can find more information about the Charlotte Mason method at CMPLENARY.COM.

Other Resources by A Charlotte Mason Plenary

The Annotated Charlotte Mason Series

Home Education—Volume 1

Parents and Children—Volume 2

School Education—Volume 3

Ourselves—Volume 4

Formation of Character—Volume 5

A Philosophy of Education—Volume 6

Original Unabridged Text by Charlotte Mason

Annotated by Rachel Lebowitz

The Plenary Plutarch Series

Plutarch's Life of Publicola: Annotated Edition

Plutarch's Life of Pericles: Annotated Edition

Plutarch's Life of Julius Caesar: Annotated Edition

Original Text by Plutarch

Annotated and Expanded by Rachel Lebowitz

Charlotte Mason Courses

Volume 6 Companion Course

CM 101 Course

Finding Your Way with Charlotte Mason's 20 Principles

Consultations

Special Needs Consultations by Amy Bodkin, EdS

CM Your Way Homeschool Consultations by Rachel Lebowitz

For a complete list of resources, or for more info about the Charlotte Mason method of education, please see A Charlotte Mason Plenary at:

CMPLENARY.COM

Made in the USA
Coppell, TX
27 May 2022

78191412R00059